The Descendants of Ann Margaret Atwood

Margaret Watson Toussaint

The Descendants of Ann Margaret Atwood

Contact information: maggietoussaint@darientel.net

Cover art by Margaret Toussaint

Muddle House Publishing
1146 Tolomato Drive SE
Darien, GA 31305

Visit us at www.muddlehousepublishing.com
First Edition © 1991, limited edition
Second Edition © 2017, Muddle House Publishing

Nonfiction
Print ISBN 13: 978-0-9967706-7-5
Print ISBN 10: 0996770674

Published in the United States of America

ACKNOWLEDGEMENTS

I could not have done this without a lot of help. For this edition, my sisters Virginia "Ginny" Baisden and Cathy Watson Glenn, helped share the genealogical research, and our Atwood cousin Johanna Kittles Williams was invaluable in her knowledge of genealogical research. Johanna kept after us to make sure we had original sources like land grants, birth records, marriage licenses, census records, death certificates, and the like.

For this first official printing but second edition of the previous family history booklet I compiled in 1991, I called upon Andrew "Drew" Parker, Suzanne Durant Forsyth, Pam Burke Fox, Claire Marguerite "Meta" Jacobs Willis, Clifford Hunter Watson, Lynn Townsend, Chris Sheffield, Patty Shuman, and Elizabeth "Beth" Walters Parker to network within their branches of the family to update the information.

Thanks to family member contributions, we've added remembrances from Bruce Ream, Priscilla Parker, and Hunter Forsyth. From the first edition, thanks go to the family members who responded to my questions about their families and their childhood: Lewis Graham, Gin Redding, Ann Burke, Sybil Baker, Marion Townsend, Gay Jacobs, and Clino Ernsberger. Thanks also go to my sister, Virginia "Ginny" Baisden, for fighting off the seed ticks in the Valona Cemetery to compile the original cemetery listing for me. I value the information everyone sent. I enjoyed learning more about our family as I put this directory together.

Every effort has been made to present accurate information. Any mistakes are mine and mine alone..

CONTENTS

1 INTRODUCTION

The other day I was reflecting that my children would never know a childhood like I had, in a place so beautiful and wild. When I tried to explain to them how it was to grow up in Valona, Georgia, they became quite confused with all of the aunts, uncles, cousins, and friends. This is my attempt to sort the people and places out in a more orderly fashion.
— Margaret Toussaint, Frederick, MD, 1991

Time marches on and twenty-five years later, we've all gotten a bit longer in the tooth. As often happens, everyone focused on their kids, grandkids, and careers, and we drifted apart. The great equalizer is funerals. Our family shows up for funerals en masse. We respect the living but we truly mourn those who have passed on.

At a cousin's funeral in 2016, my cousin Johnny Ream was heard to say, "Whatever happened to that Family History we had? We need to update it." All heads swiveled in my direction. It was on the tip of my tongue to say how busy I was with my mystery writing career, but the next words out of my mouth were "Sure."

In computer terms, 1991 was light years ago, back in the days of floppy discs for file storage. Needless to say, that digital file of the original booklet was gone. So I began retyping the pages because that was the right thing to do. That took a chunk of time and then I was ready to start collecting new information.

We have such a large family that I requested help from a point of contact in each branch. Thankfully, I was able to connect with all but one branch of the family, so I have included those updates in lineage, remembrances, and cemetery listings. In addition I tackled the challenge of recording Ann Margaret Atwood's ancestors, a process that will be ongoing for a long time due to there being so many John McIntoshes who immigrated about the same time. Best of all, through this process, I found a kindred spirit in Drew Parker, so when this edition of the family history is done, I'm officially passing the files over to him for future editions of the book.

I commend my cousin Johanna Kittles Williams who kept urging us to use original materials for the ancestral research. At her prompting, I soon abandoned trying to make heads or tails of the conflicting information in Ancestry.com. We focused on birth, death, marriage, and property records, though our task proved challenging in a local sense due to three McIntosh County Courthouse fires, which led to a lack of official records.

I've spent countless hours, along with sisters Cathy Glenn and Virginia Baisden and cousin Johanna Williams, researching our family history, sifting through published information in books and online, adding what I could verify through family records or official documents, entering the information, and proofreading. God bless genealogists (of which I am not) everywhere for their tenacity and quest for absolute proof.

This project brought many of us cousins together again. Near or far, family matters. Though we may be separated by distance, we celebrate each birth and mourn each death as deeply as if it were our own. The coast of Georgia and the sea still call to us wherever we are, and it means a lot that family still lives on some of the ancestral lands.

Though I am the author of the book for publishing purposes, I consider myself the editor or facilitator, relaying the information from the many contributors. I hope this family history brings you the same enjoyment it brought me.
— Margaret Toussaint, Darien, GA, 2017

2 FAMILY REMEMBRANCES

In collecting information for the limited edition 1991 family history, I asked my Aunt Gin (Virginia Watson Forsyth Redding) what it was like in Valona when she was growing up and if Valona was all woods at that time. The following is her response.

No it wasn't all "woods" when I was growing up! Our family owned all of Valona at one time. In fact, or as I was told, Ann McIntosh who married Henry Skelton Atwood owned from Crescent (including Oak Hill) to Carneghan (including the coastal islands Patterson and Creighton), west to the "stage road" (now called US 17). That generation lived in Eatonton where they owned interest in several plantations, mills, and a railroad, as well as large tracts in Atlanta. Sherman changed all that!

When I was a child, the only all-time residents of Valona were Gran, Mama and family, Aunt Sophie and family, and the Kittleses. The other houses were summer cottages built by family members but sold to "outsiders" . . . Where Jane Durant lived was a school house for Valona kids – that was when Lewis, Claire, Tootsie, and Bobo came up. My cousin Harold lived there for a while when I was a child. Where Conrad Rogers lives was once the family cotton gin. Y'all's house was built in Mama's yard. There were many fields and gardens. I live on one end of what was once a large field. Everyone had to have milk cows, chickens, and pigs, so a great deal of corn was planted, also enough sugar cane to make syrup. Corn was ground into grits and meal for people and Gran's deer hounds – they ate mush mixed with grease and table scraps. Gran's hands made lard, soap, and cracklings. Of course, cattle and pigs were butchered, and bacon and hams were cured and smoked for the family.

Georgia Power didn't come to the county until 1936, and the ice man only made deliveries during the summer months. Kerosene lamps and stoves, wood ranges in the kitchens, outdoor plumbing and pitcher pumps on shallow wells were what we had. Finally, Aunt Ta (Mama's sister, Clara Atwood Black) had a well drilled for Gran (Hunter and Suzanne still use it!) and we had water piped to our house and a BATHROOM.

T.P. (Thomas Perry Watson, Gin's father) was the only member of his family who did not have a college degree. Of course, he finished high school, was extremely well-read, well-mannered, and aristocratic, but I always say he was the first of the Beatniks – wanted no boss, had no ambition, or maybe even no feeling of responsibility. All he did was roam around in his launch and seine for fish. Mama, fortunately, owned land and cattle which the grocery store owner was glad to get, piece by piece, when the grocery bill couldn't be paid in cash.

The big dock in Valona was built before I was born. It was then an oyster canning plant owned and operated by cousins. Your dad's dock was built in the 1930s. Aunt Ta then owned the land and had it built for Hunter to rent. By the way, when I was a child, we would all walk down to Shell Bluff (as all of Valona was called at one time) where Aunt Sophie lived in a big two story house and the family would gather after church and dinner. Cousin Jules would have us take off our Sunday shoes and socks. He'd use dip net crabs for bass bait and he'd catch at least one, sometimes several, sea bass weighing from 20 to 50 pounds! The shore where the dock is now was then lined with large live oaks and benches, and all the way to the low water mark was like a sandy beach – no mud! (Can you imagine wading barefoot there now?)

I didn't know that Dr. Burrows was from Macon. His father, Lewis's grandfather, also Dr. Burrows, was president of the Southern Baptist Convention and the family lived on Greene Street in Augusta. His home is now marked historical. Mama met Lewis's dad while in college in Athens – Lucy Cobb – and Dr. Burrows was attending the University Dental School.

Big Mama was an accomplished pianist. She played by ear as well as by her mother's opera and classical stacks of sheet music. Her mother studied music in New York and abroad. Her mother's first husband was her German music teacher.

Swimming, aquaplaning, and family baseball games were the most fun, except for horseback riding and hunting, and of course, fishing and crabbing.
— Gin Redding, 1991

Here's what Lewis Burrows Graham said in 1991 about her family:

My father was Dr. Charles Lansing Burrows, DDS. He was living in and practicing in Nashville, Tennessee, when he died on July 23, 1907. He is buried there. Mama moved back to Valona to live in the house they built for a summer home. My fraternal grandfather was Dr. Lansing Burrows, doctor of divinity. He died October 17, 1919. My grandmother was Lulie Rochester. She died August 8, 1901, in Nashville, TN. My parents lived in Augusta, GA, for a few years.

I have many pleasant memories of growing up in Valona. We were a very close family – a lot of cousins around my age, James and Katherine Atwood, Jim and Sarah Atwood's children. They lived in a lovely two-story house in what is now known as Dunwoody Point. The house burned a few years ago. Salome, Stuart, Jane, Julie, and George Atwood were Jules and Jane Atwood's children. They lived where Rita's house is now. Ed and Bessie Atwood's children were Elliott, George, Elizabeth, Maude, Maury, Paul, Ted, and Margaret Atwood. They lived in the house that Alec and Virginia Durant bought from them. Aunt Sophie and Uncle George's children were Bob, May, Jules, Walter, Alf, Ed, Jim, and Constance Atwood. They lived in a house on the site of where Wanda lives now. (their house burned down.

A lot of people came down in the summer: the Storeys, the Dawsons, the McCathens from Waynesboro. A lot of friends lived in Crescent: the Hopkins, Grundys, and Mallards. We also had many friends from Darien. When I was a teenager, we used to have dances every Friday at the club house in Darien. The house that Bob Atwood built in Valona is part of the old club house. The diamond windows are from it too.

Mr. Tavy (Octavius) Hopkins was the caretaker on Blackbeard Island. He welcomed our house parties there. We had such fun.

We all had horses and enjoyed riding. Claire and I used to ride almost every day.

I have a picture of the old school house in Valona. I taught school a couple of years in Pineover, GA, in Jones, GA, and in Crescent City, FL, where I met my husband Ben. I was a teller in the Citizens and Southern Bank in Savannah. I was their first girl teller. I worked there two years, and then I left to get married.

Ben and I were married in 1924. We lived in Crescent City, FL, until 1945, when we moved back here and bought this place in Cedar Point. Ben came to run the factory for Hunter while he was in the Coast Guard. Rita ran it until her husband came home from the war – he was in the Philippines, but was sent to Maine, where Rita joined him. Ann was 5 years old when we moved here. Ben died in August 1974.

We never think of our children as being adopted. They are very special chosen children and are loved and appreciated more than a lot of children. The joy that they have given us is beyond comparison.

We had a very devoted mother – I often wonder how she raised nine children!
— Lewis Graham, 1991

Ann Burke responded in 1991 with memories her mother Claire had shared with her:

I remember Claire telling about sailing up the inland water route on T.P.'s yacht with Mom and all the kids when they were small (before Tootsie married at age 17). They went to FL and the St. Johns River.

I also was living on 48th Street in Savannah when your grandfather T.P. showed up again. Claire took Mom and T.P. to Ridgeland, SC, to be remarried. Must have been about 1945. I thought (along with James) he was a fascinating person – well-read and interesting to talk with – sporty clothes – I know nothing of their past history (marriage). I think they parted ways due to alcohol. I also helped get T.P. in the Marine Hospital and went to see him daily until he died. He was not with Mom very long this time as old alcohol got-in-the-way again, and she would not have that. I was in nursing school at that time, and it was so long ago, that I am a little fuzzy as to what he really died from (T.P. died of a heart attack, editor's note).

Tootsie died before Claire. Billy, Lew, and I went to her funeral. She does have Jean, Ann, and Clino surviving her. Mary died of a heart attack after Tootsie died. She was one of my favorite people.

I see my boys about once a month. Hugh is divorced and living in Jacksonville – he comes regularly for good food.
— Ann Burke, 1991

Ginny (Virginia Watson Baisden) commented in 1991 after her trip to the cemetery:

Big Gin told me that there was another family Atwood cemetery at Cedar Point. When the county cut the back road in (parallel to and behind Jane Henry and Addie Atwood's house and perpendicular to the paved road and the other dirt road into Cedar Point), the cemetery was bulldozed, pushing some of the headstones into the marsh. This is one of the main reasons why there is such a nice fence around the Valona cemetery, thanks to Big Syb and Gin.

I am swinging in the hammock on the front porch as I write this to you. A painted bunting, a chickadee, and a titmouse are visiting the bird feeder four feet away. It is high tide and the marsh is a vibrant chartreuse backdrop. Thunder is rumbling in the distance. It's a typical Saturday morning in Valona. The damn squirrels are in the pear trees, grabbing a pear, taking one bite and throwing it down. Another set of squirrels are tearing up the other bird feeder in the azaleas.

Life continues at a slower pace here. It is nice to go into a metropolitan area for the cultural advantages but it is wonderful to be able to get back here.

I am sorry that your kids, as well as Cathy's, Carol's, or for that matter, Sister's, Johnny's, Hank's, etc., will not have the opportunity growing up with a huge extended family like we did. None of the kids today will have a chance to grow up (or try to survive) in an area that allows so much freedom.

A majority of our dangers came from the environment and each other. Not from child molesters, kidnappers, spaced out junkies, etc. We had to worry more about the thrown oyster shell, BB guns, bogging without shoes, or getting your big toe

9

caught in your tricycle spokes.

TV was not a big part of life here in the 1960s. Reception was poor. Besides, who wanted to watch Lawrence Welk and Ed Sullivan anyway? The only TV worth watching was Saturday morning cartoons and Walt Disney on Sunday night.

Books have always been a part of all of our lives. Valona has been a great place to grow up if you had a little imagination. You had to be able to take a few blocks of wood and create a fleet of ships in the dirt road. . .
—Ginny Baisden, 1991

Marion Townsend contributed this in 1991 about growing up in Valona:

I have fond memories of life in Valona, and hope to have many more. As an only child, I enjoyed the company of many cousins, many of whom are still close to me. We went skiing, crabbing, fishing, and bogging at the River Bank in the summer. In the winter, we enjoyed going to get wood, oyster roasts, and marsh hen hunting.

My mother liked to get up before dawn and go to the dock and sheepshead fish. She would always bring home a string of nice ones. My dad would always be down on special occasions. He was loved by everyone in the family.
—Marion Townsend, 1991

Gay Jacobs had these thoughts in 1991 about family and Valona:

My paternal grandparents were Dr. Walter Ernest Saunders and Viola Calhoun Saunders. They are buried in Arlington, GA, along with my daddy. I was born in Quincy, FL, and Sandy and Syb were born in Tallahassee. We lived in FL where my father practiced medicine before my parents were divorced in 1945. After that, Mother, Sandy, Sybil, and I moved to Valona.

We went to school in Darien. Sandy went away to graduate high school from Emory-at-Oxford, then on to Jr. College at Norman Jr. College, Norman Park, GA, and graduate from Mercer University (Macon, GA). He lived in Stone Mountain with his wife Pam and their children. He had a real estate brokerage there. Sybil continues to live in Valona in the home of our grandmother, which was left to her. She moved back to Valona in 1978 after her divorce. Her children lived in Brunswick for a time. Karol Gay was still in high school. Perry went back to school at Brunswick College in the nursing program. Joe shrimps.

Lawrence and I lived at Cedar Point in the old two-story home behind our shrimp dock that we bought from Bobo (Hugh Burrows) in 1971, after having leased it for four years. Our eldest son, Tony, shrimped and lived in Darien for a while. At that time, Scott was shrimping out of Charleston. Meta works as a medical laboratory technologist, and lives in Valona with her husband, son Brad, and assorted animals. Laddy graduated from GA Southern in 1988 with a degree in business administration. He trained sales reps for an automotive chemical firm while he lived on St. Simons. My mother remarried for about three months to Jim Brittain who lived next door to Gin at Manchester. He was an artist and it obviously did not work out, as they were divorced the same year (1949). Mama took the name of Saunders back.

My daddy died at Heritage Inn, St. Simons Island, in 1978 of a massive heart attack. We took him to the Saunders family cemetery in Arlington, GA, for burial.

When I was a child living with Mama and Big Mama, Gin and Billy and kids lived in an old house (now torn down) next door to Bobo's house. There was no other house beyond that except Sybil and Henry's on the point. Rita lived just south of the Watson house in a frame house that burned down. On the other side of Rita's place was Jane Durant's house. It was the Valona schoolhouse (one room!) when our parents were little.

Lewis went there as a child, but Mama said the Watson group went to Darien to school. My mother had diphtheria as a child, and Big Mama taught her at home until 6th grade, as she was "delicate." Mama was salutatorian in her graduating class.

All of Big Mama's children were smart; all of them were honor graduates too. Big Hunter (Hunter Watson) was offered a scholarship to some fancy college, but he felt the family needed his earnings, so he didn't go. It was during the Depression, and money was very scarce. Big Mama was really land-poor. You know that the Meadows, where Frank Williams, Jr.'s family lives now, was Big Mama's. She had put it up for her grocery account at the old Meridian store with the understanding that she would get it back, but Mr. R.K. Hopkins, owner of the store then, refused when she had the money. Your father, Hunter, had that place picked out as his home, so then Big Mama, when Hunter married Vivian, gave him the piece of her yard that your present home is on. Big Mama and Mama told me this. Lots of her land was sold for from 50 cents to two dollars an acres. Oh well, it was the Depression, and before my time.

Big Mama had lots of papers in her house at one time about the valuable land that Gran gambled away. Big Mama and her sister "Ta" had tried to get it back (unsuccessfully), as the deed was entailed in Big Mama's grandmother's will to "go down to the children of my body" and Gran apparently had no right to dispose of it. They always said they could have gotten it back, but they would have had to prosecute their father.

Big Mama was a member of the DAR, so you can probably get at least one branch of ancestors there. I hope this is some help.
    —Gay Jacobs, 1991

Clino Ernsberger sent information in 1991 about her mother and her childhood:

My mother and father (Marie and William) were married in

Jacksonville, FL, in St. Mary's Episcopal Church with the Rev. William Wiley officiating. Mrs. Gale (nee Clino Sophia Dimitry) and Mrs. Wiley were witnesses. En route from Valona to Jacksonville, Marie was injured in a train derailment, and was hours late for her wedding. After a honeymoon in Jacksonville, they went via the steamboat Harry Lee to Georgetown, FL, where they built a home and where all their children were born. My father and his brother James were the proprietors of a wholesale seafood business and also owned extensive citrus groves on the mainland and Drayton Island.

When I was a child, all the shores of Lake George (Putnam County, FL) on the Georgetown side had wide white sand bottoms. We children loved to play in the shallow water and walk to the docks; on a little point of land under a huge cypress tree was a large sailboat turned up on its side with the broken stub of a mast buried in the sand. This was the "Virginia" on which your grandfather (T.P. Watson) had sailed from Virginia to Valona. After he and your grandmother were married, he sailed it to Georgetown, FL. Whether his wife and children accompanied him, I do not remember. I do know that the family lived at Lake George Point (Georgetown) for several years in a large two-story house. It was during this stay that my mother met my father.

Grandmother Watson was an accomplished pianist, and my mother said that often in the evenings friends and relatives would gather. She would accompany them in the singing of new and old songs. Both of my grandfathers (Burrows and Watson) had good voices.

Your grandfather, Thomas Perry Watson, was an excellent dancer. He taught my cousin Sally and I to dance on one of his visits to us.

You asked about my mother's nickname of "Tootsie". I have heard several explanations. One was that she would pretend her fist was a horn and go around tooting it all the time. Her Dad called her his "Little Tootsie" and Lewis was called "Little

Cutter" (pronounced Cooter). I assume the latter might be a nickname for a Turtle.

My mother said that when your Dad (Hunter Watson) was a baby, they had a certain large rocking chair in which she would rock him to sleep each night. As you know, automobiles were a rarity in those days, and they would pretend the rocker was a car. Each night he'd ask her to "rock me in the beel."

Clino also included a lot of detail about wedding services for Marie's descendants which I will include here.

Clino Margaret married George Richard Ernsberger of Palatka, FL, on June 22, 1935, in St. James Methodist Church, Palatka, Rev. H.A. Spencer officiating.

Ann Marie married Ocie Monroe Webb on October 4, 1969. No issue. They were married in St. Mark's Episcopal Church, Palatka, Rev. George W. Shirley officiating.

Jean Patricia married John Mason Sheffield of Ocala, FL, on June 9, 1949 in St. Mark's Episcopal Church with the Rev. W. Pipes Jones officiating.

Gale Richard Ernsberger married Betty Anne Ellett of Huntsville, AL, on September 9, 1956 in the Holmes Street Methodist Church, Rev. M.E. Coleman officiating.

Gale Richard, Jr., married Alalita Acebar Tabuena of Manilla, Philippine Islands on July 20, 1991 in the Holmes Street Methodist Church, Rev. C.E. Herring, Jr., officiating.

Dale Dimitry Ernsberger married Nancy Ellen Hunsuckle of Palatka, FL, on August 19, 1957 in St. Mark's Episcopal Church, Rev. George W Shirley officiating.

Eric Graham Ernsberger married Rebecca Cox of Tampa, FL, on April 27, 1990 in the Church of the Advent, Tampa, Rev. Henry Prior officiating.

Patricia Gale married William Foster Shuman of Atlanta, GA, on March 22, 1975 in the Gainesville Garden Center, the minister of the First Presbyterian of Gainesville officiating.

Christopher Robert married Lisa Lynn Simons of Jacksonville, FL, on September 10, 1988 in the Lakeshore Presbyterian Church.
—Clino G. Ernsberger, 1991

As the compiler of the 1991 first edition of this family history, I added my memories:

Growing up in Valona during the 1960s and the 1970s was not much different than for previous generations. Some of my generation's activities included horseback riding, crabbing, swimming, and water skiing. My favorite memories are of huge family get-togethers, such as the picnics on Blackbeard and St. Catherine's Islands, going to the Blessing of the Fleet in Darien on a Valona shrimpboat, softball games in Todd's cow pasture, and the yearly Christmas shopping trips to the B&B Variety Store in Darien with Bobo (Hugh Burrows).

I always thank my good friend Marianna Durant Hagan every time my husband tells me my Atwood blood is showing. Marianna visited us in Maryland for our children's christenings, regaling us with stories about Atwood women. She described them as being eccentric, selfish, and bossy, among other attributes. I'm not sure these are such sterling qualities, but you are what you are.

I also want to mention a family tradition from my childhood. The "Santy Claus Band" was a group of black vocalists and musicians who came by on Christmas day to sing. My recollections are from the 1960s, but I'm sure this tradition started long before then. The people in this group varied from year to year, but the central figure was a man named Snowball. He had a viola (a people-height bass instrument) strung with crabbing twine. He could play anything on that viola. Snowball's daughter had a lovely soprano voice. My cousin Hunter Forsyth would often accompany them on a piano. Oftentimes Ollie (Gay Jacobs' housekeeper) would join in the singing as well. Nobody could sing "Silent Night" like Ollie. The Santy Claus Band discontinued with the death of Snowball.

—Margaret Watson Toussaint, 1991

For the 2017 edition of the family history, several family members submitted memories. First up is an entry from Pam Burke Fox:

I have so many happy memories of Valona and Cedar Point I don't know where to begin. I guess our lives (Michael's and mine) centered around Bobo's shrimp dock where Bubba was in charge of the headers. She wore this canvas apron full of quarters and dimes. Depending on the size of the shrimp, a bucket of heads would be worth 25 cents or 35 cents. We would stand up there alongside all the headers, black ladies in white uniforms, who headed so fast you could hardly see their fingers. When we got our buckets full, we'd each take our quarters and buy drinks and moonpies from Kate, Grape Nehi for me, Orange Crush for Michael…15 cents for the drink and 10 cents for the moonpie. She made money on the deal, a nickel on each item. She sat in a lawn chair next to a red and white cooler full of ice. Those were the coldest drinks we ever had; they'd bring tears to your eyes if you drank them too fast. Kate also took us to her house to see her peacocks on occasion as a special treat. Scared the bejesus out of us the first time we heard one scream, but we were fascinated by their feathers all spread out.

The thing about Bobo's dock was that it was old. So was the rusty tub where the guys washed the shrimp when they came off the boat. Inevitably, some of those tasty treats washed right thru the drain and landed on the mud at low tide. Bubba would sent us down there to get shrimp so she could make a perloo, and we would duck walk under the dock and gather up sometimes 2 pounds of free shrimp. Bubba never had a pot to pee in or a window to throw it out of, but she was very creative when it came to economizing. — Pam Burke Fox, 2017

Hunter Forsyth took up the pen to share these remembrances:

The War Between the States left all of McIntosh County and the rest of Georgia in a state of poverty beyond belief. There was no money and most locals turned to the ocean's bounty and pine timbering for income.

This Vocational Age wasn't a happy time in the Atwood family, but learning these new skills turned out to be a blessing. There was a good living to be had from seafood and timber. With sufficient natural resources around Valona, the family survived and learned skills that were passed from one generation to the next.

During the summer of 1952, we moved from Valona to Manchester. I was nine years old. By then we had two shrimpboats, the MV Huntress and the MV Don, and Mama had started a net shop that sold netting, complete nets and doors, and miscellaneous items for shrimpboats. Daddy had a job as a heavy equipment mechanic at Camp Stewart, which is now Fort Stewart.

Somewhere around Christmas 1955, Lewis, Claire, and I were talking, and we agreed that the family had already been feeling financial hardship long before and after the Great Depression of 1929. Times were hard when I was growing up, same as when their generation grew up.

Lewis left home to find a job and landed one as a teller at a C&S Bank in Savannah. That was the first time she'd ever seen a $50 bill, much less a $100 bill. When she realized the bills were real, she got dizzy and nearly fainted over seeing those "big bucks."

Things were looking a little better financially for my family, but Daddy came home from Camp Stewart exhausted almost every day and then had to go to the dock and work on boats in order for them to go out the next morning. He'd been born with a bad heart, and in the summer of 1959 his heart gave out. He had a massive heart attack while killing a rattlesnake and was pronounced dead within fifteen minutes. It was the saddest time I had ever had to deal with.

Two years later tragedy struck again. My youngest brother, John Chisolm "Quiz" Forsyth, died in a motorcycle accident. That grief nearly tore our family apart.

Life went on, and after a few years I married the most wonderful girl I ever met, my wife of 43 years, Suzanne Durant Forsyth.

I don't want to get into my fifty-plus years of running and crewing shrimp boats. Although those were interesting times and events, it would take me another lifetime to get it all down on paper in anything resembling noteworthy format.

Today Suzanne and I still live in our cottage about forty feet from where my family's first house once stood. We would not trade places with anyone in the world because we love it here.

Valona is the same little hamlet it has always been, and we still fish off our floating dock or the shrimp docks. We still catch crabs in the creek, and local oysters and clams have made a comeback.

Around four or five Christmases ago, Suzanne gave me a baby grand piano. I keep it tuned, and she keeps it dusted, and it looks and sounds as good as new.

I usually try to be home from the dock and railway around six p.m. in order to catch the news on TV. After the news, I need a cocktail, and after the drink, a time on the piano seems in order. I don't know why I insist on the news because it does nothing but depress me. Seems like everybody hates everybody else, and all politicians are corrupt.

As I sit down on the piano bench with my drink, careful to make me a coaster, I look east toward Sapelo to watch the sunset show. Our big picture window faces east toward High Point (north end of Sapelo), but we can see across the marsh and waterways all the way to the Sapelo Lighthouse. As the sun descends, the Spartina marsh turns from a light brown to a bright golden color, and it's beautiful. To forget the discord of the news, my fingers touch the piano keys, and I play and sing the Louis Armstrong version of "What a Wonderful World."

The music swells and fills me, and I feel like the luckiest man in the world.
— Hunter Forsyth, April 2017

Cousin Bruce Ream took a stab at a remembrance:

When I was 6-7 years old, Aunt Rita-used to take me fishing all the time. She would not let me row the boat 'cause I made too much noise that scared the fish, if we had to talk it was at a whisper, also when eating our Vienna sausage and saltines again complete silence. If I happened to catch a Croaker again be very quiet even though I was very excited. We carried our drinking water in old fashion mayo glasses with metal tops, no ice right out of the kitchen spigot. No ice for the fish either, just a wet croaker sack. To this day if I am light tackle fishing I do not make a sound cause of Aunt Rita's training!

Growing up in Valona had a few drawbacks - no little baseball, football, or basketball like city kids had. Played baseball with Todd kids, only had one ball, one glove, and one very old bat. So all of us cousins fished, hunted and played in the outdoors, and summers were lots of fun. Our mother set rules for hunting and fishing, if you caught a fish no matter what it was you had to eat it, same for hunting - nothing was wasted! One time I shot 2 ducks with my single shot 4-10, I was very proud- supper on the table! Except these 2 ducks were on the very bottom of the taste scale. Plucking them and cleaning them was a pain, feathers everywhere and the breast meat was very dark. We had a cook-maid, Hanna Palmer, she knew the 2 ducks were not going to be much of a meal, she marinated them for 2 days trying to get the fishy taste to depart but nothing could help those ducks on the dinner table. Family had fried chicken and lots of vegetables, the ducks I had to eat by myself, the meat was terrible, but I ate only one and consumed all the vegetables on the table, Hana gave the other breast to our dog who was not thrilled with it either. To this day I never shot anything else but tin cans with Hunter and Sandy- fishing quickly became my salvation with Aunt Rita!!!

— Bruce Ream, 2017

Not to be outdone, Bruce's sister, Priscilla Ream Parker, weighed in on the remembrances of her childhood:

Growing up in Valona was idyllic to say the least! It was a family affair...our grandmother, Meta Atwood Watson, had nine children eight of which lived in Valona or nearby in Manchester and Cedar Point. That extrapolated to lots of aunts and uncles and cousins galore to play with! Big Mama's (as we called our grandmother) house was centrally located in a long line of her children's homes all facing east towards Sapelo. We children walked everywhere mostly barefooted - bicycles were an option but with dirt roads you'd get stuck a lot! Big Mama's house was always open to us and we'd spend great times listening to her stories! The Riverbank (our swimming hole) was directly in front of her house, which guaranteed we'd see a lot of her! The Riverbank is just a small tidal creek so we only swam at high tide - our diving board was an exposed root from the nearby oak tree. We never even gave a thought to alligators but there were probably some lurking! We were much more concerned about crabs biting our toes!

Christmas Eve in Valona was a huge event as all the men would spend days gathering wood for the biggest bonfire a little kid could ever imagine- always down by the Riverbank in front of Big Mama's! Then back to our houses where carolers – can't remember their names - with the most beautiful voices would make the rounds - we knew when they left it was time for bed so Santy Claus could come!!

Life in Valona revolved around the thriving shrimp business - just about the whole family was involved in one way or another either by owning a boat or boats or in a support position. We were all very aware of the life of a shrimper - leaving at 3 or4 a.m. and getting back twelve hours later dead tired and still the big job of unloading and all that entailed. My uncle Hunter (Big Hunter) owned the Valona Dock so a lot of the family's boats docked there including my father's boat, the *Bruce*, captained by Saul Palmer. Every boat had its own particular characteristics - all a thing of beauty to us - so you knew who was coming in way before they got close!

Our tiny post office, which was located at the Bluff next to Valona dock, had the distinction of having a female postmistress, none other than our Aunt Lewis! The P.O. was a daily stop for us kids as we got to visit with Lewis AND buy a Coca Cola and a bag of Lance salted peanuts to pour into the coke for 10 cents!!

Helicopter parenting was definitely not even dreamed of in those days of the 1950s and '60s- we were allowed to roam freely - every day was a new adventure with picnics on the flat marsh, gathering fiddlers for bait or just chasing for fun, boat trips in my cousin and best friend Ginny's boat (one trip to an island at the mouth of the Shell Bluff Creek when we were about 11 or 12 was almost the death of us as we got caught in a horrific summer storm with lightening popping all around our aluminum boat and rain filling up the boat as fast as we could bail- we pulled ourselves into the marsh and kept bailing till the storm passed- when we finally limped home hours later no one had even missed us- I think each of our mothers thought we were at the others house!!) Them were the days!!!!

Another story handed down was about our great grandfather (Big Mama's father) that everyone called Gran. He attained a substantial amount of property in the Five Points - Whitehall area of Atlanta - not sure how or why he came to own it but anyway he was involved in a poker game and his ante was the property - of course he lost it all. Just imagine what it would be worth today! Moral of that story is Don't Gamble!!

I'm sorry to say I never knew my grandfather, Thomas Perry Watson, who as the story goes sailed into Valona one day from the coast of Virginia and swept Big Mama off her feet! He was not the father or husband that Big Mama deserved so after a few kids she divorced him just to take him back and remarry and have a few more kids several years later!! Another divorce and he was never spoken kindly about that I ever heard anyway - It was like he didn't exist- I have never even seen a photo of him. I'm sure the older cousins might remember him and feel differently but in my family he was never lovingly mentioned or remembered. The good thing about him is that he fathered four wonderful unique daughters, my aunts Virginia (Gin), Margarite (Rita), Perry, and my mother, Sybil and one hero of a son, Hunter. I say hero because he became the caretaker of the family when TP disappeared. Through all the hardships of growing up in a large family with not much money and going through the depression to boot they all maintained fine-tuned senses of humor- there was always lots of laughter! Of course the family has seen its share of tragedy but thanks to Big Mama's instilling in all of us a strong sense of family, we would get through it together.
— Priscilla Ream Parker, 2017

Sliding in just under the wire, Meta Jacobs Willis, shared these fond remembrances:

I used to go visit Rita a lot when I was young. She was my Godmother – Mom named me after Claire (other Godmother) and Marguerite was from Rita…of course the "Meta" was after Big Mama's nickname. Rita and I would go fishing a lot. I especially have fond memories on cooler days of her making me hot tea with cream in it. When I think of the walk to her house from ours, I can still smell the banana shrub that was between Big Hunter's house and hers. Of course, Rita's way with words/sayings ("Rita's Idioms") always gives Scott and I a good laugh. "A flatulent (but she used the other f word) in the bush is worth two in the breeze!" What a family we have….wouldn't trade those times for anything!

Of course we have many stores, the ones told by Mammy about Big Mama's many premonitions. Here are several that I remember as a child.

1) The time Bobo and Big Hunter were hauling shrimp to "New York" (I think…) on a barge and their makeshift pilot house was a large coat they would share. Big Mama called the Coast Guard about her concerns and turned out they were in trouble as a storm had passed through.

2) The time her relative had fallen gravely ill and passed expectantly, the "old long fingered woman" appeared and was scratching the message of the death on the wall…that one still sends chills down my spine. Not sure I slept a wink the night I heard that one the 1st time.

3) The time Big Hunter saved my life when I was a toddler. Apparently Scott and I had taken off to the Riverbank (swimming hole in front of Big Mama's house). Scott said I walked in and the current got me, I don't remember but he joked that he pushed his little sister in! Scott realizing this wasn't good started screaming and thankfully Big Hunter heard him. Adults always can decipher a child's scream for help vs. scream when playing. He ran down and pulled me out.

A funny one to me was when my cousin Tom Crawford went around painting things in Valona. He painted Big Hunter's door and funniest to me was Tony's new red little Chevy....the paint was light blue from leftover shrimp boat bottom paint! Tom was just beautifying the neighborhood!!

Of course, the crabbing times at "Yellow tail" creek with Mammy, the mud bogging through the marsh, jumping off the shrimp boats on incoming tide to swim around to the River Bank (to me the initiation to the 'Valona older group'), Marion taking us to the Riverbank at low water to play (had partial white sand at the Riverbank bottom back then), the horses getting loose and Big Hunter thinking it was a huge man in his yard but it was our old horse "Tex", riding horses with friends and all the cousins – Tony, Scott, Ben, Suzanne, Christie and Mary Alice, going out in Mary Alice's "glass bottom" small boat at Manchester and loosing Gin's outboard motor accidently (Jiggs tied the motor on after recover/repair of that ole motor), our pet pig "Petunia" that was later given away to Dad's parents for Pork Chops we felt (Tony had a few choice Valona words when Petunia was taken away, and we never ate Pork Chops at Granny Jacobs house again), the weekend softball games at Bruce and Pat's (all of Valona grown and young were included), and one of my all-time favorites was Christmas when "Snowball" came from house to house singing Christmas Carols – Lil Hunter would always play the piano and join in the celebration! Everyone would pretty much follow them to each house through Valona. Good, Good times!!

I wouldn't trade the memories for anything.
—Meta Willis, 2017

Valona, relatively speaking (1991 edition)

George and John Atwood were twin brothers who were born on January 1, 1849. They married LaRoche sisters in a double wedding. John's wife passed, and he married her sister a few years later. Descendants of both lines are double related.

George E. Atwood and Sophia LaRoche had the following children: Constance, May, Jules, Walter, Alf, Ed, Jim, and Robert (Bob) Atwood.

Constance suffered a bad fall as a child and was paralyzed on one side. She did not marry.

Cousin May is the Kittles connection. She is the mother of Big Peter, Big George, and Billy Kittles.

Bob (Robert Atwood) had several children, of whom I only personally knew his daughter, Wanda. She married Owen Hunter and their children were Woody and Ann Hunter. Woody is married and has a family in Atlanta, while Ann married and had a daughter, Melissa Sykes, and a granddaughter named Emmaline.

George and Sophie's other children married and settled in Valona and became the families of Jim and Sarah Atwood, Jules and Jane Atwood, and Ed and Bessie Atwood. Lewis Graham's essay has more details about these extended family members.

John McIntosh Atwood, referred to by our family as Gran, married Maria LaRoche and their daughter, Clara Atwood Black, is known in the family as Aunt Ta. After Maria passed away, Gran married her sister, Clara, and they had three children: Ann Margaret, Maria Livingston, and Elizabeth King.

Ann Margaret Atwood went by Meta but the entire family

called her Big Mama. She married twice, each union producing offspring. Her first husband was dentist Dr. Charles Lancing Burrows, and her second husband was Thomas Perry Watson. Ann Margaret's children were Marie "Tootsie" Lansing Burrows, Lewis Gibson Burrows, Claire Rochester Burrows, and Hugh Atwood Burrows. Her Watson children were Hunter "Big Hunter" Atwood Watson, Marguerite "Rita" Atwood Watson, Virginia "Gin" Elizabeth Watson, Perry Francis Atwood Watson, and Sybil "Big Syb" Atwood Watson.

Maria Livingston Atwood married A.H. Brown with no issue. Maria died of tuberculosis in her 20s.

Elizabeth King Atwood (Lizzie, born 1878, died 1882, 3 years and 10 months old) died of diphtheria. She was the daughter of John McIntosh Atwood and Clara LaRoche Atwood.

As mentioned briefly in Gay Jacob's remembrance, Gran (John McIntosh Atwood) was the red-headed relative who reputedly lost the family's real estate holdings in what's now Peachtree Street in downtown Atlanta during a card game. (More about that in Section 7 of this book.)

However, this is controversial even in our family. Aunt Gin told me that she thinks Gran probably sold it because he couldn't pay the taxes the Yankees imposed after the war. Gin said Big Mama (Ann Margaret Atwood) and her sister, Aunt Ta (Clara Atwood Black), appealed all the way to the Supreme Court (because Gin typed the correspondence) to no avail even though it was entailed property.

William Henry Atwood, George and John Atwood's brother, was a Captain during the War Between the States. His son, Mac Atwood, is Adeline "Addie" Atwood Hubbard's father. This line of Atwoods became 1991's Cedar Point Atwoods.
— Margaret Toussaint and Virginia Baisden, 1991

3 FAMILY BRANCHES

Descendants of ANN MARGARET ATWOOD
b. 1876   d.1957   Note: Meta, Big Mama

Married   **Dr. Charles Lansing Burrows**
Date August 1, 1895   b. 1869   d.1907   Note: Dr. Burrows was a dentist in Nashville, TN; he died of tuberculosis

(1)   MARIE LANSING BURROWS
b.1896   d.1979   Note: Tootsie, Mimi

(1)   LEWIS GIBSON BURROWS
b.1898   d.1995   Note: died at 97 as nation's oldest postmistress

(1)   CLAIRE ROCHESTER BURROWS
b.1900   d.1980

(1)   HUGH ATWOOD BURROWS
b.1903   d.1975   Note: Bobo

Married   **Thomas Perry Watson**
Date March 6, 1908   b.1876   d.1950   Note: Big Mama and TP separated several times

(1)   HUNTER ATWOOD WATSON
b.1909   d.1978   Note: Big Hunter

(1) MARGUERITE ATWOOD WATSON
b.1912   d.1989   Note: Rita

(1) VIRGINIA ELIZABETH WATSON
b.1915   d.2000   Note: Gin

(1) PERRY FRANCIS ATWOOD WATSON
b.1918   d.1991

(1) SYBIL ATWOOD WATSON
b.1920   d.2010   Note: Syb, Big Syb

Numbers in parenthesis indicate generations from Ann Margaret Atwood

(1)   Descendants of **MARIE LANCING BURROWS**
b.1896 d.1979 Note: Mariel, Tootsie, Mimi

Married **William Dimitry Gale**
Date 1915 b.1884 d.1950

(2) CLINO MARGARET GALE
b.1915   d.2000   Note: Johnson-Overturf Funeral Home, Palatka, FL handled the arrangements
(2) ANNE MARIE GALE
b.1917 d. 2003 Note: married Ocie Monroe Webb, no issue
(2) CAROLINE CELESTE GALE
b.1919 d.1919 Note: died at birth
(2) LOIS CLAIRE GALE
b.1921 d.1924
(2) MARY ADELAIDE GALE
b.1923 d.1987 Note: unmarried, no issue
(2) WILLIAM DIMITRY GALE
b.1925 d.1925 Note: lived one day
(2) JEAN PATRICIA GALE
b.1926 d.2008

(2) Descendants of **CLINO MARGARET GALE**
B.1915 D.2000
Married **George Richard Ernsberger**
Date 1935 b.1913 Note: Dick
(3) GALE RICHARD ERNSBERGER
b.1936 Note: Ike
(3) DALE DIMITRY ERNSBERGER
b.1940 d.2013

(3) Descendants of **GALE RICHARD ERNSBERGER**
b.1915 d.2000 Note: Ike
Married **Betty Anne Ellett**
Date 1935 b.1935
(4) DEBORAH ANNE ERNSBERGER
b.1958 Note: Debbie
(4) MARGARET ELLEN ERNSBERGER
b.1961 Note: Maggie
(4) GALE RICHARD ERNSBERGER, Jr.
b.1962 Note: married Analita A. Tabuena in 1991

(3) Descendants of **DALE DIMITRY ERNSBERGER**
b.1940   d.2014
Married   **Nancy Ellen Hunsuckle**
Date 1957   b.1939
(4) ERIC GRAHAM ERNSBERGER
b.1972   b.1972   Note: m. Rebecca Cox 1990, (4) son Casey
Graham Ernsberger b.1991
(4) DAVIN BRANT ERNSBERGER
b.1975

(4) Descendants of **ERIC GRAHAM ERNSBERGER**
b.1972
Married **Rebecca Cox**
Date 1990
(5) CASEY GRAHAM ERNSBERGER
b.1991

(2) Descendants of **JEAN PATRICIA GALE**
b.1926   d.2008   Note: Riverside Memorial Park, Jacksonville,
FL
Married   John Mason Sheffield
Date 1949   b.1923
(3) PATRICIA GALE SHEFFIELD
b.1950
(3) WILLIAM LANSING SHEFFIELD
b.1956   Note: Lanse
(3) CHRISTOPHER ROBERT SHEFFIELD
b.1962

(3) Descendants of **PATRICIA GALE SHEFFIELD**
b.1950
Married   **William Foster Shuman**
Date 1975   b.1927   d.1991
(4) JENNIFER GALE SHUMAN
b.1976
(4) ELIZABETH MARIE SHUMAN
b.1985   Note: Beth

(3) Descendants of **CHRISTOPHER ROBERT SHEFFIELD**

b.1962   Note: Chris
Married   **Lisa Lynn Simon**
Date 1988   b.1969
(4)   JUSTIN ALEXANDER SHEFFIELD
b.1990
(4) LAURA GALE SHEFFIELD
m. **Eric Bond** Dec. 5, 2015
(4) JOSH SHEFFIELD

Numbers in parenthesis indicate generations from Ann Margaret Atwood

(1)   Descendants of **LEWIS GIBSON BURROWS**
b.1898   d.1995

Married   **Benjamin Hawkins Graham**
Date 1924   b.1990   d.1974
(2)   ANN DOUGLAS GRAHAM
b. 1938   d.2003   Note: adopted
(2)   BENJAMIN WAYNE GRAHAM
b.1955   d.2017   Note: adopted from Ann and Wayne Pack, no issue
(2)   ANN CHRISTINE GRAHAM
b.1956   d.2017   Note: Adopted from Ann and Wayne Pack, no issue

(2)   Descendants of **ANN DOUGLAS GRAHAM**
Married   **George Richard Everett**
(3)   VIRGINIA LEIGH EVERETT
b.1961
(3)   ANITA ELIZABETH EVERETT
b.1962
(3)   AMY CATHERINE EVERETT
b.1966
(3)   GEORGE RICHARD EVERETT
b.1968

(3)   Descendants of **ANITA ELIZABETH EVERETT**
b.1962
Married   **Lee Consolatore**
(4)   VALERIE ANN CONSOLATORE
b.1986
(4)   AMY CONSOLATORE
b.1988
(4)   LEE ANTHONY CONSOLATORE
b.1989

(3)   Descendants of **AMY CATHERINE EVERETT**
b.1966
Married   **Michael Canning Murphy**
Date 1991
(4)   MICHAEL CANNING MURPHY
b.1986

(2)   Descendants of **ANN CHRISTINE GRAHAM**
b.1956   d.2017
Married   **Robert Lee Walters**
Date 1976   Note: died
(3)   MARY ELIZABETH WALTERS
b.1978   Note: Beth
Married   **John Browning**
Date 1981   Note: died, no issue
Married   **Charles Byerly**
Note: No issue, divorced
Married   **Gerald "Jerry" Lane**
Note: no issue

(3)   Descendants of **MARY ELIZABETH WALTERS**
b.1978   Note: Beth
Married   Ryan Andrew Parker
Date 2016
(4)   SHELBY ANN GALE
b.1999   Note: father is Michael Brian Gale, but no marriage
(4)   GRAHAM CONNER WALTERS
b.2006

Numbers in parenthesis indicate generations from Ann Margaret Atwood

(1) Descendants of **CLAIRE ROCHESTER BURROWS**
b. 1900   d. 1980   Note: Bubba

Married **James Harden Barfield**
Date 1921   b. 1900   d. 1950   Note: divorced 1942

(2) JAMES RICHARD BARFIELD
b. 1928
(2) ANN ATWOOD BARFIELD
b. 1930
(2) HUGH BURROWS BARFIELD
b. 1932 d. 1985?

Married   **Gerald J. Ford**
b. 1900   d. 1976   Note: Gerry

(2) Descendants of **JAMES RICHARD BARFIELD**
b. 1928
Married **Ann Guerard**
Date 1951   b. 1928
(3) JAMES RICHARD BARFIELD, III
b. 1952   Note: Jimmy
(3) WILLIAM HUGH BARFIELD
b. 1955   d. 1977   Note: no issue
(3) VIRGINIA ANN BARFIELD
b. 1958   Note: Gigi

(3) Descendants of JAMES RICHARD BARFIELD
b. 1952   Note: Jimmy
Married   **Sandra Chord**
Date 1987   Note: divorced
Living with Martha (20 years or so)

(3) Descendants of **VIRGINIA ANN BARFIELD**
b. 1958   Note: Gigi
Married   **John Harrison**
Date 1977   b. 1956
(4) LAUREN GALE HARRISON
b. 1980
Married   Jeffery S. Opar
b. 1978

(4) HILLARY HOPE HARRISON
b. 1982
Married Gerald Sherman Palmer, Jr.
Date 2011 b. 1982

(2) Descendants of **ANN ATWOOD BARFIELD**
b. 1930
Married William Leon Burke, Jr.
Date 1951 b. 1923 d. 1989 Note: Billy
(3) PAMELA CLAIRE BURKE
b. 1951
(3) MICHAEL WILLIAM BURKE
b. 1953 d. 1997 Note: traffic accident
(3) DAVID ANTHONY BURKE
b. 1957
(3) WILLIAM LEON BURKE, III
b. 1958 Note: No issue

(3) Descendants of **PAMELA CLAIRE BURKE**
b. 1951
Married **James Russell Fox**
Date 1974 b. 1947
(4) JESSAMYN BURKE FOX
b. 1980
(4) TRAVIS JAMES FOX
b. 1987

(3) Descendants of **MICHAEL WILLIAM BURKE**
b. 1953 d. 1997 Note: traffic accident
Married **Robin**
d. 1999 Note: liver failure
(4) **SHANE MICHAEL BURKE MAPP**
  b. 1994 Note: Shane was 3 when Michael died and 5 when
Robin died. He was adopted by his older half sister and her
husband, Celica and Robbie Mapp

(3) Descendants of **DAVID ANTHONY BURKE**
b. 1957 Note: No issue
Married **Donna Rayburn**
Date 1988 b. 1963 Note: Divorced
Married Rhonda Holland

(3) Descendants of **WILLIAM LEON BURKE, III**
b. 1958   Note: No issue
Married **Gloria Burton**
Date 1990   b. 1952

(2)   Descendants of **HUGH BURROWS BARFIELD**
b. 1932
Married   **Ruth Parkinson**
Date 1963 Note: Divorced in 1966
(3) REBECCA DIANNE BARFIELD
b. 1964   Note: Becky

(3) Descendants of **REBECCA DIANNE BARFIELD**
b. 1964   Note: Becky
Married   **Eric Williams**
Date 1985 Note: divorced in 1966
(4) MEGAN WILLIAMS
b. 1987
(4) JAMES R WILLIAMS
b. 1989

Numbers in parenthesis indicate generations from Ann Margaret Atwood

(1)   Descendants of **HUGH ATWOOD BURROWS**
b. 1903   d. 1975, Note: Bobo

Married   Louree McQuaig
Note: divorced, no issue divorced, no issue

Married   Francis Redding
b. 1906   d. 1979   Note: no issue.

Numbers in parenthesis indicate generations from Ann Margaret Atwood

(1)   Descendants of **HUNTER ATWOOD WATSON**
b. 1901   d.1978   Note: Big Hunter

Married **Vivian Virginia Decker**
Date: 1944   b.1926   d.2010 Note: divorced 1969
(2)   CATHERINE LOUISE WATSON
b.1946   Note: Cathy
(2)   CAROLYN HELEN WATSON
b.1947   d. 2012   Note: Carol
(2)   SANDRA VIRGINIA WATSON
b.1950   Note: Ginny
(2)   MARGARET LEIGH WATSON
b.1955
(2)   CLIFFORD HUNTER WATSON
b.1960   Note: Cliff

(2)   Descendants of **CATHERINE LOUISE WATSON**
b. 1946   Note: Cathy
Married   **Paul Mallard Glenn**
Date 1965
(3)   HUNTER WATSON GLENN
b.1969
(3)   SHANNON PATTERSON GLENN
b.1971
(3)   LUKE WATSON GLENN
b.1979   d.2011   Note: US Navy 2000-2004

(3)   Descendants of **HUNTER WATSON GLENN**
b.1969
Married   **Keryl Leah Mitchell**
Date 1992   b.1970   Note: divorced 2015
(4)   LINDSEY LEAH GLENN
b.1992
(4)   LOGAN ELIZABETH GLENN
b.1993

(3)   Descendants of **SHANNON PATTERSON GLENN**
b.1971
Married   **Steven Michael Smith**
Date 2002   b.1970

(4)   DALTON GLENN SMITH
b.2005
(4)   CATHERINE SMITH
b.2010

(3)   Descendants of **LUKE WATSON GLENN**
b.1979   d.2011   Note: ashes on St. Catherine's Island Beach,
Ga., and in St. Andrews Cemetery, Darien, Ga.
Married   **Rachel Ann Martinez**
Date: 2000   b.1980   Note: divorced
(4)   NOAH GLENN
b.2000
Married   **Misty Lynn Nolan**
Date 2008   b.1979
(4)   HOLDEN HUNTER NOLAN GLENN
b.2008

(2)   Descendants of **CAROLYN HELEN WATSON**
b.1947   d. 2012   Note: Carol
Married   **Michael John Gorby**
Date 1974   b.1945   Note: divorced
(3)   **JASON HUNTER GORBY**
b.1978
(3)   **BRIAN MICHAEL GORBY**
b.1982   Note: Married **Yoann Roman** 9/14/2015

(2)   Descendants of **SANDRA VIRGINIA WATSON**
b.1950   Note: Ginny
Married   **George Henry Baisden**
Date 1970   b.1901   d.1985   Note: no issue

(2)   Descendants of **MARGARET LEIGH WATSON**
b.1955
Married   **Craig Robert Toussaint**
Date 1976   b.1949
(3)   SUZANNE CHRISTINE TOUSSAINT
b. 1980
(3)   MICHELLE LEIGH TOUSSAINT
b.1982

(3)   Descendants of **SUZANNE CHRISTINE TOUSSAINT**
b.1980
Married   **Ryan Patrick Phillips**
Date 2002
(4)   BENJAMIN ALLEN PHILLIPS
b.2010
(4)   ABRAHAM CRAIG PHILLIPS
b.2012
(4)   ANNALIESE MARGARET PHILLIPS
b. 2014

(3)   Descendants of **MICHELLE LEIGH TOUSSAINT**
b. 1982
Married   **Zachary Thomas Adams**
Date 2007   b.1983
(4)   HUNTER NICHOLAS ADAMS
b.2010
(4)   SAVANNAH LEIGH ADAMS
b.2012

(2)   Descendants of **CLIFFORD HUNTER WATSON**
b.1960
Married   **Sonja Ann Rasmussen**
Date 1984   b.1958
(3)   AMELIA KATHERINE WATSON
b.1993
(3)   WILLIAM HUNTER WATSON
b.1996   Note: Will

Numbers in parenthesis indicate generations from Ann Margaret Atwood

(1)   Descendants of **MARGUERITE ATWOOD WATSON**
b.1912   d.1989   Note: Rita

Married   **Thomas Crawford Brooks**
Date 1942   b.1918   d.1981   Note: TC, divorced
(2)   MARION BLACK BROOKS
b.1947   d.2006

(2)   Descendants of **MARION BLACK BROOKS**
b.1947   d.2006?
Married   **H. Lynn Townsend**
Date 1965   b.1942
(3)   THOMAS CRAWFORD TOWNSEND
b.1970   Note: Tom Crawford
(3)   IRVIN BROOKS TOWNSEND
b.1974   Note: Brooks

(3)   Descendants of **THOMAS CRAWFORD TOWNSEND**
b.1970   Note: **Tom Crawford**
Married

(3)   Descendants of **IRVIN BROOKS TOWNSEND**
b.1974   Note: Brooks
Married
(4)   RILEY TOWNSEND
b.2006
(4)   COLBY TOWNSEND
b.2008

Numbers in parenthesis indicate generations from Ann Margaret Atwood

(1)   Descendants of **VIRGINIA ELIZABETH WATSON**
b.1915 d.2000 Note: Gin

Married **William McClellan Forsyth**
Date 1937 b.1912 d.1959 Note: Billy

(2) DONALD MCCLELLAN FORSYTH
b.1940 d.2008 Note: Don
(2) HUNTER WATSON FORSYTH
b.1943 Note: Little Hunter
(2) JOHN CHISOLM FORSYTH
b.1947 d.1961 Note: Quizzom, no issue
Married **George Yeomans Redding**
Date 1963 Note: Jiggs, divorced, no issue

(2) Descendants of **DONALD MCCLELLAN FORSYTH**
b.1940 d. Note: Don
Married Mary Lou Jackson
Date 1961 Note: divorced
(3) **MARY ALICE FORSYTH**
b.1962 Note: Mary Alice

Married **Jane Williamson Durant**
Date 1969 Note: divorced
(3) JOHN CHISOLM FORSYTH
b.1970 Note: Johnny

Married **Linda Mock Summer**
Date 1979 Note: divorced
(3) DONALD RICHMOND FORSYTH
b.1980 Note: Donnie

(3) Descendants of **MARY ALICE FORSYTH**
b.1962 Note: Mary Alice
Married **Bud Thomas**
Note: divorced
(4) JACKSON THOMAS

(3) Descendants of **JOHN CHISHOLM FORSYTH**
b.1970 Note: Johnny
Married **Ann Wilson**

Note: divorced
(4) EMMA HOUSER FORSYTH
b.2000
(4) KATHRYN MCGREGOR FORSYTH
b.2000   Note: Katy
(4) ABIGAIL WILLIAMSON FORSYTH
b.2005   Note: Abby

(2) Descendants of **HUNTER WATSON FORSYTH**
b.1943
Married   **Suzanne Rice Durant**
Date 1974   b.1957
(3) WILL ATWOOD FORSYTH
b.1975

(3) Descendants of **WILLIAM ATWOOD FORSYTH**
b.1975   Note: Will
Married   **Joanna Riley**
b.1975   Note: divorced
(4) JOSEPH ALEXANDER RILEY FORSYTH
b.2010   Note: Joe Alex
(4) LENA ATWOOD MAPLES-FORSYTH
b.2011   Note: mother's name is **Kristy Maples**
(4) GREY COOPER MAPLES-FORSYTH
b.2016   Note: mother's name is **Kristy Maples**

Numbers in parenthesis indicate generations from Ann Margaret Atwood

(1) Descendants of **PERRY FRANCIS ATWOOD WATSON**
b. 1918   d. 1991   Note: Perry

Married   **Dr. Irwin Jasper Saunders**
Date 1939   b. 1917 d. 1978
(2) GAY CALHOUN SAUNDERS
b. 1940
(2) ALEXANDER HALL SAUNDERS
b. 1941   d. 2016   Note: Sandy
(2) SYBIL WATSON SAUNDERS
b. 1944   Note: Syb

(2) Descendants of **GAY CALHOUN SAUNDERS**
b.1940
Married   **Lawrence Francis Jacobs**
Date 1956   b. 1936
(3) LAWRENCE ANTHONY JACOBS
b. 1957   d. 2009   Note: Tony
(3) DOUGLAS SCOTT JACOBS
b. 1958   Note: Scott
(3) CLAIRE MARGUERITE JACOBS
b. 1960   Note: Meta
(3) LAWRENCE FRANCIS JACOBS, JR.
b. 1963   d. 2016   Note: Laddy

(3) Descendants of **LAWRENCE ANTHONY JACOBS**
b. 1957   d. 2009 Note: Tony
Married   **Deborah Seely**
Date 1985   Note: Debbie, divorced
(4) MARLANA CALHOUN JACOBS
b. 1988   Note: Marly
(4) SARAH ELIZABETH JACOBS
b. 1993

(3) Descendants of **DOUGLAS SCOTT JACOBS**
b. 1958   Note: Scott
Married   **Virginia Kittles**
Date 1979 Note: divorced
(4) VIRGINIA MARGUERITE JACOBS
b. 1982
(4) KATHRYN MARIE JACOBS

b. 1985

(4)   Descendants of **VIRGINIA MARGUERITE JACOBS**
b. 1982   Note: Gina
Married   **Brady Charles White**
Date 2016   b. 1981
(5) **AVA GRACE WHITE**
b. 2017

(4)   Descendants of **KATHRYN MARIE JACOBS**
b. 1985   d. Note: Kate
Married   **Scott Michael Baker**
Date 2010   b. 1980
(5) **ALEXANDRIA JUNE BAKER**
b. 2014   Note: Alex

(3)   Descendants of **CLAIRE MARGUERITE JACOBS**
b. 1960   d. Note: Meta
Married   **James Edward Willis**
b. 1952
(4)   BRAD WILLIS
b.1998

(3)   Descendants of **LAWRENCE FRANCIS JACOBS, JR.**
b. 1963   d. 2016   Note: Laddy
Married   **Elizabeth Gerson**
Date 1991   Note: divorced

(2)   Descendants of **ALEXANDER HALL SAUNDERS**
b. 1941   d. 2016 Note: Sandy
Married   **Pamela Wightman**
Date 1970   Note: Pam
(3)   ANNE MARGUERITE SAUNDERS
b. 1979

(3)   Descendants of **ANNE MARGUERITE SAUNDERS**
b. 1979
Married **John Cooper Padgett**
Date 2001 b. 1979   Note: divorced
(4) **PERRY SHYANNE PADGETT**

b. 2001   Note: Shyanne
(4) **SKYLAMARIE CAROL SAUNDERS**
b. 2007   Note: Skyla

(2) Descendants of **SYBIL WATSON SAUNDERS**
b. 1944   Note: Syb
Married **Farris Harper Clinard, III**
Date 1967   Note: Butch, divorced
(3) PERRY SAUNDERS CLINARD
B. 1968.   Note: Little Perry
(3) JOSEPH MCPHERSON CLINARD
b. 1970   Note: Joe
(3)   KAROL GAY CLINARD
b. 1973   d. 2011   Note: Karol Gay

(3) Descendants of **PERRY SAUNDERS CLINARD**
b. 1968   Note: Little Perry
Married   **James Mincy**
Date 1985   Note: Divorced
(4)   SYBIL MARGUERITE CLINARD
b. 1986   Note: Megan
(4)   AARON BRADY CLINARD
b. 1989
Married   **David Brannen**
Date   Note: divorced
(4)   DAVID BRANNEN
b. 1993
Married **Will White**
Date
(4)   PATRICK WHITE
b. 2000

(3) Descendants of **JOSEPH MCPHERSON CLINARD**
b. 1970   Note: Joe
Married   **Lydia**
Date 1990   Note: Divorced
(4)   JAMES CLINARD
b. 1991
Married   **Tammy Shuman**
Date   Note: divorced
(4) DANIEL LAWRENCE CLINARD

b. 1999

(3) Descendants of **KAROL GAY CLINARD**
b. 1973   d. 2011   Note: Karol Gay
Married **Matthew Roberts**
Note: divorced
(4)   MATTHEW ROBERTS
(4)   TREVOR ROBERTS
(4)   RAYNE ROBERTS

Numbers in parenthesis indicate generations from Ann Margaret Atwood

(1)   Descendants of **SYBIL ATWOOD WATSON**
b.1920   d.2010   Note: Big Syb

Married   **Henry Putnam Ream**
Date 1942   b.1914   d,1962

(2)   ROBERT BRUCE REAM
b.1942   Note: Bruce
(2)   JOHN ATWOOD REAM
b.1946   Note: Johnny
(2)   PRISCILLA ANNE REAM
b.1950   Note: Sister
(2)   HENRY PUTNAM REAM, Jr.
b.1957   Note: Hank

Married   **Albert Brewer Baker**
Date 1966   b.1915   d.1982   Note: no issue

(2)   Descendants of **ROBERT BRUCE REAM**
b.1942   Note: Bruce
Married   **Patricia Geiger**
Date 1967
(3)   ROBERT BRUCE REAM
b.1971   d.1974
(3)   RICHARD HENRY REAM
b.1976
(3)   JOHN MORGAN REAM
b.1977

(3)   Descendants of **RICHARD HENRY REAM**
b.1976
Married   **Kate Mitchell**
Date 2014   b.1984
(4)   REAGAN ELIZABETH REAM
b.2015

(3)   Descendants of **JOHN MORGAN REAM**
b.1977
Married   **Jennifer Allison Drummond**

Date 2004   b.1978   Note: Jenny
(4)   LILLIAN MARIE REAM
b.2007
(4)   CAROLINE SYBIL REAM
b.2009
(4)   GEORGIA NOLAN REAM
b.2014

(2)   Descendants of **JOHN ATWOOD REAM**
b.1946   Note: Johnny
Married   **Vickie Boland**
Date 1969   Note: divorced
(3)   ANTHONY ATWOOD REAM
b.1964   Note: Tony
Married   **Karen Stickle**
Date 1985
(3)   ARTHUR PUTNAM REAM
b.1986   Note: Putnam
(3)   PRISCILLA CLAIRE REAM
b.1988   Note: Claire

(3)   Descendants of **ANTHONY ATWOOD REAM**
b.1964   Note: Tony
Married   **Dana Hamilton**   Note: divorced
(4)   PRISCILLA ROSE REAM
b.2004

Married   **Lisa Knight**
Date 2013
(4)   SHAYLA BELLE
b.2008   Note: Daughter to Lisa Knight, adopted by Tony in 2016
(4) STORM
Note: Son to Lisa Knight, not adopted by Tony

(3)   Descendants of **PRISCILLA CLAIRE REAM**
b.1988   Note: Claire
Married   **Zachary John Meyerkord**
Date 2015   Note: Zak
(4)   JOHN WATSON MEYERKORD
b.2016   Note: JW

(2)   Descendants of **PRISCILLA ANNE REAM**
b.1950   Note: Sister
Married   **James Philip Parker**
Date 1973   b.1948   Note: Jimmy
(3)   SYBIL ANNE PARKER
b.1977   Note: Sybi
(3)   JAMES ANDREW PARKER
b.1978   Note: Drew

(3)   Descendants of **SYBIL ANNE PARKER**
b.1977   Note: Sybi
Married   **Matthew Gregory Kuchar**
Date 2003   b.1978   Note: Matt
(4)   CAMERON COLE KUCHAR
b.2007
(4)   CARSON WRIGHT KUCHAR
b.2009

(3)   Descendants of **JAMES ANDREW PARKER**
b.1978   Note: Drew
Married   **Annie Jane Wood**
Date 2002   b.1978
(4)   JAMES ROBERT PARKER
b.2009
(4)   ANNETTE PRISCILLA PARKER
b.2012

(2)   Descendants of **HENRY PUTNAM REAM**
b.1957   Note: Hank
Married **Elizabeth King**
Date 1981   Note: Liz
(3)   HENRY PUTNAM REAM, III
b.1983   d.2002   Note: no issue
(3)   JENNIFER HAMILTON REAM
b.1985
(3)   WILLIAM HARDIN REAM
b.1990   Note: Will

*Numbers in parenthesis indicate generations from Ann Margaret
Atwood*

4 ANCESTORS OF ANN MARGARET ATWOOD

Since my sister Ginny and I began this genealogy quest with our grandmother Ann Margaret Atwood Burrows Watson as the starting point, then her ancestors might be assigned negative numbers or we could start the numbering over. Math isn't my strong suit, so forget those negative numbers!

Assuming our paternal grandmother is now generation number 1, the others generations back into time are successive generations removed from Ann Margaret.

(1) Ann Margaret Atwood Burrows Watson, born 1876, died 1957, two husbands, and nine children. Her husbands were Dr. Charles L. Burrows, dentist, and Thomas Perry Watson, adventurer. Her descendants are the subject of this family history.

Ann Margaret's parents were (2) John McIntosh Atwood (born 1849, died 1930) and his second wife (2) Clara Francis LaRoche (b.1849, d.1891).

(2) Clara LaRoche's parents were (3) James Archibald LaRoche (born 1811, died 1899, buried at Cedar Point) and (3) Mary Magdalene Gibson (born 1810, died 1887, also buried at Cedar Point in McIntosh County, GA). Clara's

paternal grandparents were (4) Isaac LaRoche (born 1783, died 1822, married 1809, buried in Augusta, GA) and (4) Elizabeth Sophia McIntosh Oliver (born 1784, died 1859). Elizabeth's parents were (5) William Gibson (died 1830) and (5) Mary Madeleine Fatio (born 1778, died 1820; first married to George Fleming and had one child, Mary Fleming, who married Davis Floyd of GA). Mary Madeleine's parents were (6) Louis Philip Fatio (died 1799 of plague) and (6) Ann Douglas (died 1788 of a strep throat). Louis' parents were (7) Francis Phillippe (born in Switzerland, died 1810; of Italy) and (7) Marie Magdalena Crispel, daughter of Signore Louis Crispel of Nice, Italy. Ann Douglas' father was (7) Col. John Douglas of England. (This information from a typed booklet in our family "The Atwood Family and Allied Families." This booklet references: Vol. I Record of Service of Connecticut Men in the Revolution, compiled by Authority of The General Assembly, Hartford 1889; Vol. II War of 1812; Vol. III Mexican War; Vols. I. II, and III all in one book; Atwood, Elisha (page 468, Vol I), Corporal Aug. 12. Discharged Sept. 14, Col Dunning's Co. – 5th, 13th Regiment of Militia at NY in 1776; the DAR papers of Julie Olin Atwood aka Mrs. Marion Hagan; and "The First Hundred Years" by Temple, page 114.)

(2) John McIntosh Atwood's parents were (3) Henry Skilton (also spelled Skelton in places) Atwood (born 1795 in Watertown, CT, died 1864 in Cedar Point, GA, married in Savannah, GA on December 7, 1824) and (3) Ann Margaret McIntosh (born Aug. 5, 1807 and died 1893 in Cartwright, GA, which is in Putnam County). Within his large family, John had a twin brother named George Elliott Atwood (born 1849 and died 1914). His other six siblings were Ruth Ann (married William Elliott Dunwoody), Jane Margaret Atwood, James Alfred Atwood, Matilda Alethia Atwood, Davis Atwood, and William Henry Atwood. Some interesting notes: both John and his twin George married LaRoche sisters. When John's first wife (Maria LaRoche) passed, he married a third LaRoche daughter, Clara Francis LaRoche. So all descendants of John and George are double cousins. Also of interest, John and George had a double wedding on Jan

4, 1870 (John's marriage to Maria LaRoche). John was known as "Gran" and John McI. (This information also in "The Atwood Family and Allied Families")

Growing up we also heard that John McIntosh Atwood was the relative that had gambled away family holdings in the downtown Atlanta area. However, in looking through family papers for this second edition of our family history, we found a handwritten note about this transaction (see Section 7). Gran had okayed a relative to sell a property of his in that area, and the relative sold all of the adjacent properties as well, pocketing the money.

(3) Henry Skilton Atwood's parents were (4) Elisha Atwood (born 1745 and died 1825) and (4) Mary Skilton (born 1746 and died 1830). The Atwood lineage is well researched on both sides of the marriage.

(4) Elisha Atwood's parents were (5) Oliver Atwood (born 1717 and died 1810) and (5) Lois Wheeler (born 1716, death date unknown). Oliver's parents were (6) Jonathan Atwood (b1675 and died 1733) and Sarah Atwood (born 1684 and died 1728). Sarah's parents were (7) Roger Terrill of England (born 1649 and died 1722) and (7) Sarah Lester (born 1653 and died 17_1). Sarah Lester's parents were Roger Terrill of England (b. 1616) and Abigail Terrill (born 1621 and died 1692). Returning to (5) Lois Wheeler, her parents were (6) John Wheeler III and (6) Ruth Wheeler (no birth or death dates for the Wheelers was found).

(4) Mary Skilton Atwood's parents were (5) Henry Skilton of England (born 1718 and died 1802 in CT) and Tabitha Skilton (born 1717 and died 1797 in CT), married July 9, 1741. Tabitha Skilton's parents were (6) Joseph Avery (1692-1753) and Tabitha Gardiner Avery (born between 1685 and 1690 and died 1753). Joseph Avery's parents were (7) Capt. James Avery, Jr. (born 1646 and died 1728) and (7) Deborah Avery (born 1648 and died 1729). Capt. James Avery, Jr.'s parents were Capt. James Avery, Sr., (born 1621

and died 1700) and Joanna Greenslade Avery (born 1622 and died 1693) Deborah Avery's parents were (8) Edward Stallyon (born 1623) and (8) Margaret Mary Elizabeth Stallyon (born 1627 and died 1680). (5)Tabitha Avery's parents were (7) William Gardner (born 1670) and Elizabeth Wilkinson.

(3) Ann Margaret McIntosh's parents were (4) John Lachlan McIntosh (born 1778 and died 1801) [Note: there are at least three John Lachlan McIntoshes in coastal Georgia during this time period. This John Lachlan is not the one who died in Savannah in 1826] and (4) Margaret McCullough (born 1785, died 1810 in McIntosh County). [Note: after Margaret McCullough passed, John Lachlan married Agnes Harrell, daughter of William and Mary Harrell. Meanwhile, Ann Margaret was three when her mother died, and she was raised by her paternal grandmother Ann McKenzie below] Margaret McCullough's ancestry wasn't found in our family papers or any online source, however, John Lachlan McIntosh's parents were (5) John McIntosh (too many John McIntoshes in this cohort to be certain of the birth or death year); and (5) Ann McKenzie (born 1733 and died 1833 at age 100 at Cedar Point, GA, in McIntosh County). Ann McKenzie's parents were (6) Donald McKenzie (born 1715 in Scotland and died at Oak Hill Plantation in McIntosh County, Ga, date not found) [Note: he was given a King's Land Grant for Oak Hill, which covered most of the high land between Crescent and Meridian, including Valona, GA] and (6) Mary Merriman [Note: Mary was the daughter of an English officer, her lifespan dates were not found, but she reportedly came to GA with the family of General Oglethorpe.]

Where does this confusion about the two John McIntoshes leave us?

Growing up in Valona, my sisters and I often heard that we were descended from Scottish Highlanders. Some relatives claimed we came from the noted John Mohr

McIntosh. We never doubted that for a second.

[Note: John Mohr McIntosh (1700-1761) was a direct descendant of the McIntosh Clan Chiefs of Scotland and was one of the first Scots to pioneer in coastal GA. He came to America on the *Prince of Wales*. The ship left Inverness, Scotland in October 1735, captained by George Dunbar, and landed first in Savannah in January 1736 and later reached Darien on February 1, 1736. John Mohr arrived with 44 men, 20 women, 25 boys and 17 girls. Shortly after their arrival in Darien, another ship of Scotsmen came with more of their kinsmen. John Mohr commanded General James Oglethorpe's Highland Independent Company of Foot, and along with Indians from the Creek and Cherokee nation, defeated the Spanish invasion. His son and nephew served General Washington in the Revolutionary War. Two descendants, George McIntosh Troop and Thomas Spalding, became governors of Georgia.]

However, as my sister Ginny and I researched this "fact" we learned that hearing a story handed down through generations isn't the same as proving it. For one thing, families recycle names, and our extended family seems particularly fond of the names John, Ann, and Margaret. We tried and tried to find a connection to John Mohr McIntosh, but for starters, there were four John McIntoshes on the *Prince of Wales*. At the particular junction where we got stuck, in the mid-1700s, it could be one of those Johns or another one altogether.

We thought sure it would be so easy, perhaps as simple as checking Ann Margaret Watson's DAR entry form. However, she used her Atwood lineage to establish one of her relatives was a Patriot in the Revolutionary War. Atwood family lineage is well documented back to the early 1600s.

With that a dead end for divining an answer to "how do we connect to John Mohr McIntosh" question, we turned to other branches of the family for answers. Turns out that at least two cousins descended from our great grandfather's twin brother were fed the same story in their formative years, that of being related to John Mohr McIntosh. I requested the lineage from their records, and it didn't match what we'd uncovered in our family papers.

Buddy Sullivan, our local historian and a cousin of sorts, noted that he didn't believe our branch of the family descended from the John Mohr McIntosh line and suggested we might look into the John Benjamin McIntosh line. John Benjamin McIntosh, another esteemed branch of that illustrious family, also came over on the *Prince of Wales*. More about this later.

Cousin Johanna Kittles Williams searched records to identify our John McIntoshes in the early to mid-1700s. The more she dug, the more she confirmed what we'd long suspected: published genealogy records don't support a clear familial lineage connection to any known John McIntosh. We looked in the DAR archives, at the online records of the Church of the Latter Day Saints, at census records, at findagrave.com, in various books of the time, as well as Ancestry.com.

Johanna found a court decision online (see Sources, *Reports of Cases*) where John Lachlan McIntosh's second wife, Agnes Harrell McIntosh Smith, sued the executor of John Lachlan's estate, Henry Atwood, over marital property. The case records confirm the lineage of John McIntosh marrying Ann McKenzie and fathering John Lachlan McIntosh. Specific facts in the case: John McIntosh (d1801, will recorded 1826) married Ann McKenzie and had one son John Lachlan McIntosh. John Lachlan married Margaret and had a child named Ann Margaret. After Margaret died in 1810, John Lachlan married (Oct. 1810) Agnes Harrell and there was no surviving issue. John Lachlan McIntosh died 1820. His daughter Ann Margaret McIntosh married Henry Atwood in 1823. In 1825, Henry became executor for John Lachlan McIntosh's estate. Ann McIntosh died 1833. The suit of Agnes Smith vs Henry Atwood was filed in 1848, it went to the Ga. Supreme Court, and Henry Atwood prevailed.

However, even with this confirmation of our proposed lineage, trying to find two specific John McIntoshes in a sea of John McIntoshes in the 1700s proved daunting. Since we had part of the puzzle extending up from Ann Margaret, my gggrandmother, surely we could build down from John Mohr McIntosh to connect, or at least that's what we thought as we dove into this rabbit hole of genealogy using online resources.

POSSIBILITY ONE: In one online source (RootsWeb, McCullum Family), we found reference to John Mohr McIntosh's son, John McIntosh, born 1728 in Borlum, Inverness, Scotland and died 1796 in Jamaica (we dubbed him Jamaica John). He is listed as being the son of John Mohr McIntosh (b 1698 in Inverness Burgh, Inverness-shire Scotland) and Margaret Marian McGillivray (born 1703). (Note: John Mohr's wife is listed nearly universally as Margery Frazier, so that's one strike against credulity for this source.) [According to Buddy Sullivan's *Early Days on the Tidewater* and other sources, this John McIntosh (born 1728) left GA in 1752 and moved to Jamaica. He died there 44 years later in Dec 1796.] But, getting back to our family's genealogy puzzle, a John McIntosh married Ann McKenzie (b1733 d1833) of Cedar Point, McIntosh County, GA. Their son is John Lachlan McIntosh. If Jamaica John were our ancestor, that would establish a connection to John Mohr McIntosh and his life in Jamaica would explain the lack of records here. Since there's no separate confirmation of this information, we're hesitant to consider it seriously. I found reference of John McIntosh living in Jamaica in his later years. He is listed as an overseer of Flower Hill Plantation in St. James, Jamaica, for several years in the 1790s and listed as "single."

POSSIBILITY TWO: In checking online records to determine whether Ann (also seen as Anna) McKenzie's father was named Daniel or Donald, I came across a John Lachlan McIntosh (born 1778 and death unknown) whose father John McIntosh (1757-1792; son of General Lachlan McIntosh and Sarah Threadcraft) was born in Darien and died at Frederica Plantation on St. Simons Island, GA March 15, 1792. This record stated that John Lachlan McIntosh was married to Margaret McCullough and the father of Ann Margaret McIntosh, which fits our known ancestors. However, this red herring sent me on a several hour long journey into the life of Revolutionary War hero, General Lachlan McIntosh, his wives, and his children. There are more than fifty versions of this family's matrimonies and descendants. This John McIntosh, son of General Lachlan, not to be confused with his more famous brother Col. "Come and take it" John McIntosh, does not seem to be an acclaimed soldier and is not often remarked or noted on many of these family trees. I found differing mentions of him in five family trees at Ancestry.com before I stopped looking, though I'd probably scanned at least twenty family trees. If he married into our family, all the official records (birth, death, marriage license, property deeds) are buried deep.

OTHER LESS POSSIBLE JOHN MCINTOSHES:

JOHN HOUSTON MCINTOSH – not our John
John Mohr's son George McIntosh (born 1739 and died 1779) married Ann Priscilla Houston (born 1744 in Savannah, GA), daughter of Sir Patrick Houston. Their children included John Houston McIntosh (born 1753 and died 1836; also seen as b.1764 d.1848), Elizabeth Eliza Bayard Clinch (born about 1775 and died 1848), and Catharine Ann McIntosh Sadler (born about 1775). John Houston McIntosh married Mary Randolph and their children were Gen. Bayard Livingston Mcintosh (b.1836) and Mary Randolph Kilgour (b.1841). Children of the daughters wouldn't have the McIntosh surname, so this line of inquiry was abandoned.

LT COLONEL JOHN MCINTOSH and JOHN NASH

MCINTOSH – not our Johns

John Mohr McIntosh's sons included Colonel William McIntosh who married Mary Mackay. Their son Lieutenant Colonel John McIntosh (born 1748, died 1826) married Sarah Swinton and they had a son John Nash McIntosh who married Sally Ann Rokenbaugh of Harpers Ferry, VA. John and Sallie also had a son named John, John McQueen McIntosh. None of these names or their descendants connect with our known lineage.

CAPTAIN JOHN MCINTOSH – not our John

Lt. John Benjamin McIntosh, born 1686 in Scotland and died 1740 in Savannah, son of Brigadier Gen. Wm McIntosh and Mary Reade, married Catherine, daughter of Angus McIntosh of Holm, on April 17, 1711. On the *Prince of Wales* passenger manifest he's listed as John McIntosh, age 50, of Dores, farmer. His wife Catherine was age 45 at the time. Their children were Elizabeth (age 20), Jannet (age 18), Lachlan (age 12), John (age 21), and Roderick (age 19 and of the Highland Rangers). John Benjamin farmed what is now current day Belleville in McIntosh County, GA. His son, Captain John McIntosh, born 1715 in Scotland and died 1787, married Margaret "Mary" McGillivray. Their children were William McIntosh of Mallow (1745-1794) and Catherine Troup. William married Sevoy, II, Marchand of the Creek Indians, had several children before returning to McIntosh County and marring Barbara (born 1760). In Ancestry.com in the Williams Family Tree, William is shown with two sons named John McIntosh (1784-1842) and John McIntosh (no dates given) who lived in McIntosh County, but there is no spouse or descendants listed for either John. It may also be a duplication error and there is just one son of William named John McIntosh. Either way, the trail turned cold. (Note: I wanted to believe this lineage was correct because my father, Hunter Watson, always said there was Indian blood in the family – but it was not to be.)

In conclusion, we were unable to establish a direct connection with the John Mohr McIntosh lineage, the

Brigadier General William McIntosh line, or that of the John Benjamin McIntosh line. The information on John Lachlan McIntosh marrying Margaret McCullough feels solid as it is confirmed through several online sources. We cannot say with any certainty whether we are descended from the more distinguished McIntoshes, from the lowliest person in the clan, or from somewhere in between.

Our amateur investigation was fraught with conflicting information reported by various families in Ancestry.com. We tried to rely on birth records, DAR records, headstones from FindAGrave.com, census data, and other official documents, but the information from 300 years ago was scarce at best. In addition, the Atwood Cemetery at Cedar Point was bulldozed to make a road and the cemetery records for that site show six graves remaining, three of which are unmarked. Further complicating our search was the burning of the McIntosh County Courthouse in 1863 (during the Burning of Darien in the Civil War), 1881, and 1931.

With regret, Ginny, Cathy, Johanna, and I threw in the towel on this ancestor search. Perhaps the next generation will have more luck than we had in establishing the exact McIntosh connection. However with at least four to five generations forward from Ann Margaret McIntosh Burrows Watson known, and four to seven generations back from her also identified, we think that's not too shabby for amateur genealogists.

5 ATWOOD CEMETERY LISTINGS AUGUST 2017

ATWOOD CEMETERY
Valona, GA

Location: From Darien, GA, junction of US Hwy. 17 and GA Hwy 99, take GA Hwy 99 9.2 miles north. Turn right onto Valona Road. In 0.2 miles, cemetery is on your right.

"The Atwood family owned land from Cedar Point through Valona. George Elliott Atwood, son of Henry Skelton and Ann McIntosh Atwood, owned a large portion of Shell Bluff, present day Valona. He had a ship chandlery there in the 1880s. In circa 1890 he designated land for a family cemetery. The location was chosen for its higher elevation. The Atwood family has traditionally valued marshes and rivers-the cemetery has a salt marsh on one side and a creek on another. Atwood Cemetery, burial ground for the Atwoods and their descendants, is beautifully maintained." —History of the Atwood Cemetery, as seen in *Cemeteries of McIntosh County*, Georgia, Lower Altamaha Historical Society, 2000, edited by Mattie R. Gladstone, page 29.

(Note: listings as of May 2017 reported in rows from northwest corner to southwest corner, starting at Valona Road side of cemetery)

Row 1:
Mary Alice Evans Sikes
b. 4/12/1928   d.2/13/1995

David Martin Sykes
b.8/16/1955   d.12/11/2000

Edna Dent Kittles McKnight
b.11/1/1913   d.7/14/1990

Barbara S. Kittles
b.4/3/1936   d.12/19/2007
Wife of William H. Kittles

William H. Kittles
b.5/4/1935   d.4/29/2011

Deborah A. Kittles Wallace
b.8/23/1956   d.5/4/2011
Mother of Shawn and Dylan

Row 2:
Mattie Perrin Atwood
b.10/31/1885   d.10/25/1960
Wife of Elliott McIntosh Atwood

Elliott McIntosh Atwood
b.2/8/1884   d.2/15/1942

William David Hubbard
b.11/13/1912   b.8/21/1988
LT SG USN Atlantic & Pacific Theater WWII
Husband of Addie Atwood

Margaret Lafitte Kittles Berge
b.9/3/1912   d.10/30/2009
Wife of Carl Berge

Carl Wilhelm Berge

b.2/2/2014 d.1/24/2005
Husband of Margaret, Father of Peggy, Grandfather of Maggie;
friend of Jorge

Robert Black Atwood, Jr.
b.7/4/1933 d.11/28/2006

Kenneth Paul Atwood
b.5/12/1960 d.11/3/2004

Row 3:
George E. Atwood
b.1/1/1849 d.5/21/1914

Sophie Lachlan LaRoche Atwood
b.2/21/1851 d.1/24/1930
Married George E. Atwood on Jan. 4, 1870

Constance Atwood
b.1/25/1897 d.1/11/1966

Mrs. W.W. Atwood
b.1889 d.1966
Metal H.S.

James Roger Atwood
b.unknown d.10/18/1912
Age 35 years

Capt. W.H. Atwood
b.9/7/1836 d.6/4/1912
Confederate Veteran
Husband of Tallulah Butts

Tallulah Butts Atwood
b.10/5/1850 d.10/17/1871
Wife of Capt. W.H. Atwood, married 10/5/1850

Sibyl Atwood
b 2/15/1890 d 4/21/1919

Atwood Hudson, PhD
b.11/29/1901   d.3/3/1993

Daniel B. Hudson
b.12/17/1907   d.12/4/1978
Capt. US Army   WWII

Ruth Bryan Hudson, CLU
9/29/1905   d.8/21/1991

Donald Bryan Hudson
b.12/5/1938   2/3/1993
Journalist

Louise M. Atwood Hudson
b.7/11/1868   2/12/1930
Wife of R.P. Hudson

Robert Patrick Hudson
b.2/16/1879   d.9/27/1936
Husband of Louise M. Atwood

Row 4:
Martha LaRoche
b.2/13/1846   d.1929

Vivian LaRoche
b.2/29/1908   d.12/1919

Row 5:
Gerald J. Ford
b.3/31/1900   d.3/6/1976
1st LT US Army   WWI & II

Claire Burrows Barfield Ford
b.10/31/1900   d.11/25/1980

Daughter of Ann Margaret Atwood & Dr. Charles Lansing Burrows

William Hugh Barfield
b.7/10/1955   d.11/18/1977

Zachary T. Williams
b.9/14/1994   d.12/1/1995
Grandson of Hugh Barfield and Ruth Parkinson Joyner

Hugh Burrows Barfield
b.3/26/1932   d.8/28/2000
US Coast Guard 1952-1960

Carolyn Watson Gorby
b.2/2/1947   d.9/15/2012
Mother of Jason Hunter and Brian Michael Gorby

James Edward O'Kelley
b.1/30/1937   d.2/14/2016

Vivian Decker Watson O'Kelley
b.5/14/1926   d.11/27/2010

Row 6:
Robert Bruce Ream, Jr.
b.1/16/1971   d.2/13/1974
Son of Robert Bruce Ream and Patricia Ream

Marie L. Brown
b.1/16/1875   d.3/11/1905
Wife of A.H. Brown

John McIntosh Atwood
b.1/1/1849   d.10/20/1933
Twin brother of George E. Atwood

Clara LaRoche Buchman Atwood
b.1849   d. 1891

unmarked, between her husband John and daughter Ann Margaret

Ann Margaret Watson
b.12/18/1876   d.8/7/1957
Daughter of Clara LaRoche and John M. Atwood
Wife of Dr. Charles Lansing Burrows and Thomas Perry Watson
DAR marker

Hugh Atwood Burrows
b. 6/20/1903   d.7/4/1975

Francis Redding Burrows
b.1/21/1906   d.7/11/1979
Wife of Hugh Atwood Burrows

Thomas Perry Watson
b.12/27/1876   d.3/3/1950

Hunter Atwood Watson
b.3/13/1909   d.1/26/1978
BMI US Coast Guard WWII
Son of Ann Margaret and Thomas Perry Watson

Marguerite Watson Brooks
b.7/17/1912   d.4/23/1989
"Rita"

Marion Brooks Townsend
b.2/15/1947   d.12/28/2006
Wife of H. Lynn Townsend

Row 7:
James L. Atwood
b.1/16/1873   d.11/20/1913

Willard Nutting Atwood
b.4/10/1902   d.1/23/1908

Son of John L. and Sarah D. Atwood
Grandad's angel

Row 8:
Virginia Watson Forsyth Redding
b.8/3/1915   d.11/28/2002
Wife of William W. Forsyth and George Y. Redding
Mother of Donald M. Forsyth, Hunter W. Forsyth, and
John C. Forsyth

William McClellan Forsyth
b.11/25/1912   d.6/20/1959
CM3 USNR WWII

John Chisolm Forsyth
b.2/15/1947   d.6/27/1961
Son of Virginia Watson and William McClellan Forsyth
"Mr. Quizzom"

Row 9:
Henry Putnam Ream
b.10/16/1914   d.4/6/1962
Born in New York, died Sea Island, GA
Husband of Sybil Atwood Watson

Sybil Watson Ream Baker
b.1/1/1920   d.6/22/2010
Born in Valona, GA, died on Sea Island, GA
Wife of Henry Putnam Ream and Albert Brewer Baker, Jr.
Mother of Robert Bruce Ream, John Atwood Ream,
Priscilla Ream Parker, and Henry Putnam Ream, Jr.

Albert Brewer Baker, Jr.
b.12/21/1915   d.6/5/1982
Born Baltimore, MD, died Sea Island, GA
Husband of Sybil Watson Ream Baker

Weslie Ann Parker
b.4/21/1926   d.3/3/2003

Born in Ailey, GA, died on St. Simons Island, GA

Row 10:
Alexander Hall Saunders
b 10/5/1941   d.7/31/2016
"Sandy"
Husband of Pamela Wightman Saunders
Father of Anne Margerite Saunders

Karol Gay Clinard Roberts
b.8/3/1973   d.9/20/2011
Daughter of Ferris Clinard, III, and Sybil Hillis
Mother of Mathew, Trevor, and Rayne
Sister of Perry White and Joseph H. Clinard

Perry Watson Saunders
b.7/28/1918   d.7/20/1991
Daughter of Thomas Perry and Ann Margaret Watson
Mother of Gay, Alexander, and Sybil

Lawrence Anthony Jacobs
b.1/10/1957   d.6/25/2009
"Tony"
Son of Lawrence and Gay Jacobs
Father of Marlana Calhoun and Sarah Elizabeth

Allison Bradley Jacobs
b.7/22/1941   d.5/17/2009
Chief Master Sargent
Loving brother and uncle

Lawrence Francis Jacobs, Jr.
b.3/24/1963   d.7/17/2016
"Laddy"

Lewis Burrows Graham
b.1898   d.1995
Wife of Ben Graham

Benjamin H. Graham
b.8/2/1900 d.8/14/1974

Benjamin Wayne Graham
b.4/1/1955 d. 1/26/2017

Christie Graham Lane
b.7/29/1956 d.2/21/2017
Wife of Gerald "Jerry" Lane, mother of Beth Walters Parker

Unmarked grave listed in *Cemeteries of McIntosh County,*
p. 30.
Amelia Catherine Cleland
b.12/26/1869 d.12/22/1899
Wife of George W. Cleland
Daughter of James and Sarah Nafew Davis Brown

Buried nearby in Valona on Home Place
Howard Owen Hunter
b.8/13/1922 d. 6/7/1983 1st LT USAF WWII
Husband of Wanda Atwood Hunter
"Owen"

Wanda Atwood Hunter
b.12/7/1923 d.1/8/2017
Wife of Howard Owen Hunter

6 PHOTOS AND FAMILY DOCUMENTS

Ann Margaret "Meta" Atwood Watson with Quiz Forsyth

Hunter Watson and mother Meta Watson about 1925 in Georgetown, FL

Meta Watson and children, 1936. From left, Luree Burrows, Hugh Burrows holding Little Hugh, Ann Burke (child), Perry Saunders, Gin Redding, Meta Watson, James Barfield with ball, Claire Ford, Sybil Ream, Lewis Graham, Ben Graham, and Hunter Watson

About 1950, from left, Sandy Saunders with dog, Hunter
Forsyth behind him, Johnny Ream, Little Syb, Cathy Watson,
Marion Brooks, Carol Watson, Quiz Forsyth. Adults from left,
Perry Saunders, Rita Brooks,
and Meta Watson

Meta Watson (Big Mama) and Marion Brooks, granddaughter

**Meta Watson and granddaughter Ginny Watson,
about 1954**

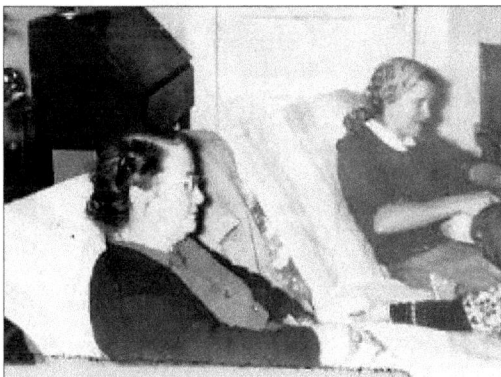

From left, Meta Watson and daughter Sybil Watson

Perry Watson

From left, Sybil Watson and Gin Watson in Valona

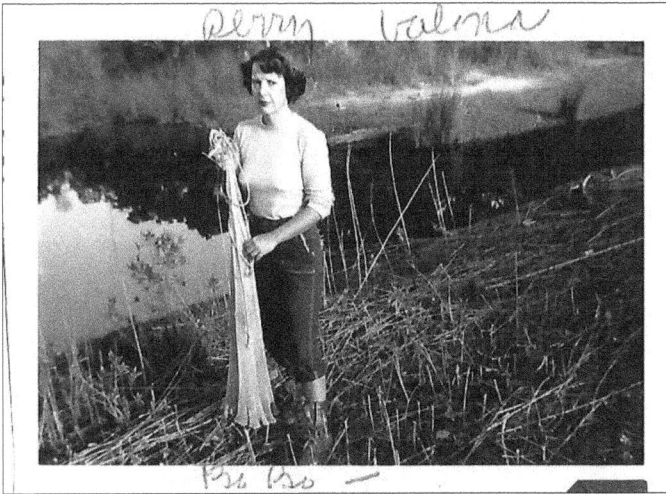

Perry Watson in Valona about 1953

"Little" Hugh Burrows and Claire Burrows

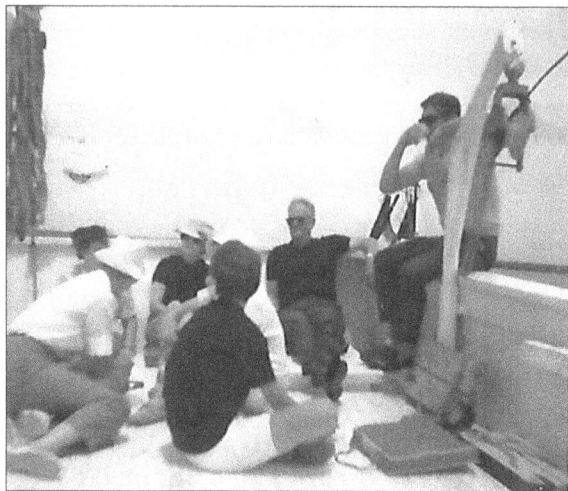

Hunter Watson, right rear in dark shirt

Gerry Ford and Gay Saunders about 1950

**Sybil Ream, her son Johnny Ream, and Gin Forsyth
at Syb's, Thanksgiving 1959**

**Jiggs Redding, T.C. Brooks, father of Marion Brooks
(far right), on St. Simons Island**

Sybil Saunders at Big Mama's house, Valona

Sandy and Gay Saunders

Bruce Ream, Sandy Saunders, and Hunter Forsyth

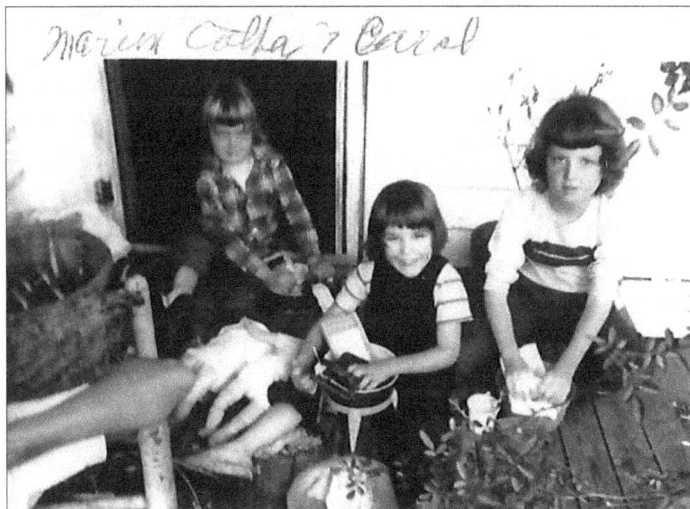

From left, Carol Watson, Marion Brooks, Cathy Glenn

Bruce Ream, Ann Burke, and Don Forsyth

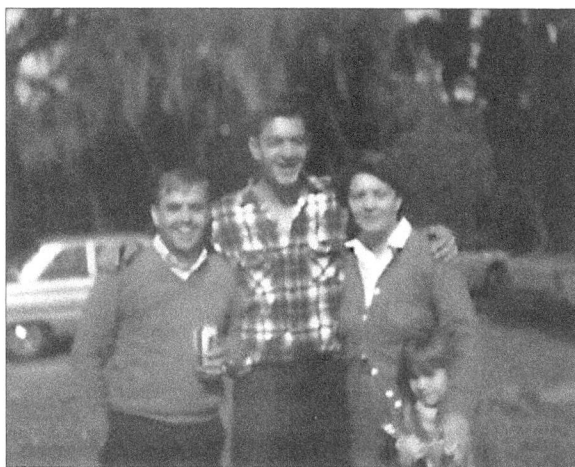

From right, Sandy Saunders, Hunter Forsyth, Rita Brooks, and Meta Jacobs, Christmas 1966

From left, Lynn and Marion Townsend, George and Mary Kittles, Hugh "Bobo" Burrows, and Hunter Forsyth

Marion Townsend and son Tom Crawford Townsend

From left, sisters Sybil and Perry Watson, Gerry Ford (Claire's husband), and Meta Watson

From left, Claire Ford, Don Forsyth, and Hunter Watson

**From left, Hunter Watson, Claire Ford,
Hugh "Bobo" Burrows, and Hugh's wife Francis Burrows**

**From left, front: Sandy Saunders, Bruce Ream,
Johnny Ream, Quizzom Forsyth, Hunter Forsyth, Don
Forsyth; back, Henry Ream, Ann and James, Gay Saunders,
Perry Saunders, Gin and Billy Forsyth, and Jiggs Redding**

From left, Gin Forsyth and Francis Burrows

**From left, Don Forsyth with his uncles,
Hunter Watson and Hugh "Bobo" Burrows**

From left: standing, Perry Saunders, Sybil Ream, Henry Ream, Francis Burrows, Jerry Ford, Gin Redding; sitting, Rita Brooks, Hunter Watson, Claire Ford, Meta Watson, Hugh Burrows

The Darien High School Eighth Grade Class of 1923--Identified as much as possible by Bill Haynes, a member of this class. Pictured left to right, back row, Tom Durant, Joe Whitesides, Archie—, Miss Day, Lee Proffitt, Bill Haynes, Hunter Watson. Front row, Addie Atwood, Lottie Johnson, Elizabeth Forbes, Fannie McDonald and Ethel Rogers. (Photo courtesy of William G. Haynes, Jr.)

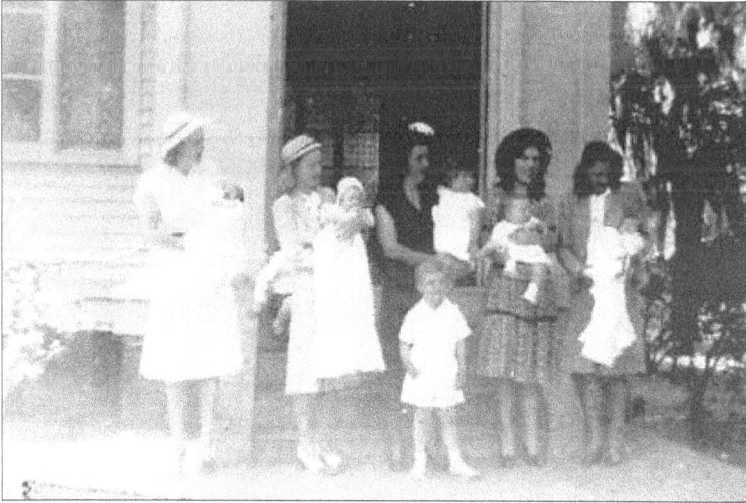

Family christening on Easter, April 5, 1947. From left, Gin Forsyth and Quizzom, Sybil Ream with Johnny, Perry Saunders holding Little Syb with Sandy standing, cousin Wanda Atwood with Woody, and Rita Brooks with Marion.

Meta Watson with Gerry Ford

From left, sisters Perry and Sybil Watson

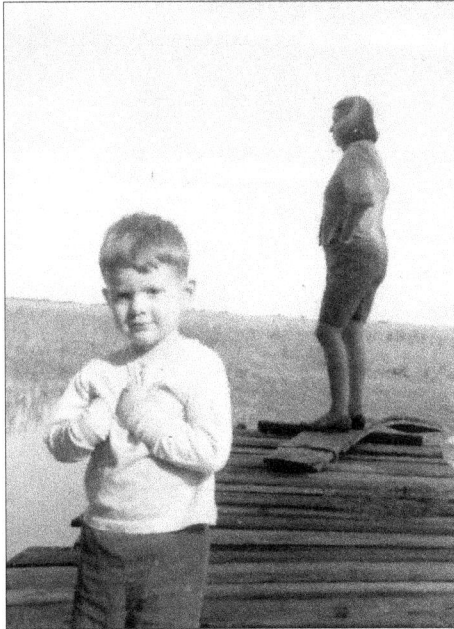

Laddy Jacobs with his Mammy, Perry Saunders, at the Valona Riverbank

Front left, Hunter Watson in the Coast Guard

Hunter Watson at Valona Dock, 1940s

About 1952, Hunter Watson's shrimpboat, the Chief, being
built in Valona between the homes of Meta Watson and
Hunter Watson. They're rolling the boat on timbers
down to the Riverbank to launch it.

Cathy Glenn's husband Paul found this in his travels.
The Chief was one of Hunter Watson's former boats.

Sybil Watson and Henry Ream engagement photo, 1941

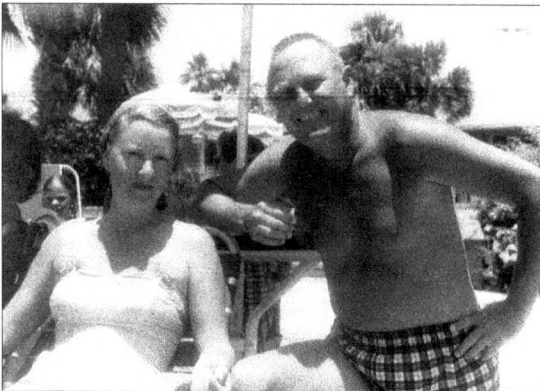

Sybil and Henry Ream, 1961 at the Beach Club

From left, Carol Watson, Marion Brooks, Pauline Pelham (?), Quizzom with tongue out, Johanna Kittles, and Johnny Ream

Uncle Walter Meyers and Hunter Watson at the Bluff

A gaggle of bridesmaids from a womanless wedding put on by the Darien school system. Photo IDs are from Johanna Kittles Williams. From left, Charlaine something or somebody Carnegie, Johanna Kittles, maybe Helen Cowart, Sandra Williamson, possibly a Rozier, Nell Buchanan, Angelina Valentie, unknown, and Cathy Watson.

From left, Beth Parker, her mother Christie Lane, Lewis Graham, and Christie's brother, Ben Graham

From left, Priscilla Ream, Marion Brooks, and Johnny Ream

Lewis Graham was the oldest postmistress in the US when she died at age 97. At her death, the Valona Post Office closed and residents had to get their mail in nearby Meridian.

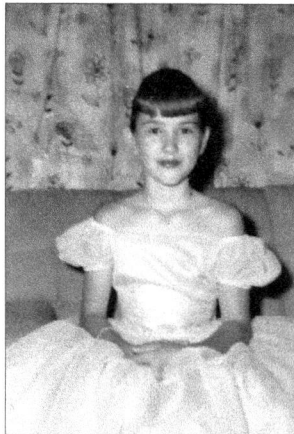

Marion Brooks at piano recital

**Back row from left: Ginny, Carol, and Cathy Watson.
Front row, Marion Brooks**

Quizzom Forsyth with Pat Norris

From left, Margaret and Cliff Watson, then Tony, Scott, and Meta Jacobs, about 1963

1967 confirmation picture. Children, front row from left, Marianna Durant, Margaret Watson; back, Kit Hawthorne, Christie Graham, Ben Graham, and Meg Williams

Margaret Watson, Valona, 1957

Queenie the horse. From left, Marianna Durant, Margaret Watson, Ann Hunter, and Suzanne Durant. Early 1960s

Hunter Forsyth, a fine pianist and vocalist

Ginny Baisden practices her cast net skills, about 2008

**The Watson Girls, about 2007. From left, Cathy Glenn,
Ginny Baisden, Margaret Toussaint, and Carol Gorby**

**This boat came into the Watson family in the 1960s.
It was named for Hunter Watson's children,
Cathy, Carol, and Cliff. As of 2017, the Three Cees
is still trawling the local waters.**

OYSTER FACTORY   VALONA, GA.

**1906 Shell Creek Canning Company at site of
current Durant dock in Valona.**

Marie Lancing Burrows Gale, oldest daughter of Ann Margaret Atwood Burrows Watson, lived in Florida after her marriage. The image far left is Marie at age 63. The center image is dated circa 1945 when she was 49, and the last is dated 1977 when she was 81. She resided in Georgetown and later in Palatka, until her death on July 20, 1979. Known as Mariel and Tootsie to her siblings, Marie was called Mimi by her family.

Marie Lancing Burrows Gale and her husband, William Gale, about 1940s.

Mary Adelaide Gale (1923-1987) didn't marry or have children. She was Marie B. Gale's 4th child.

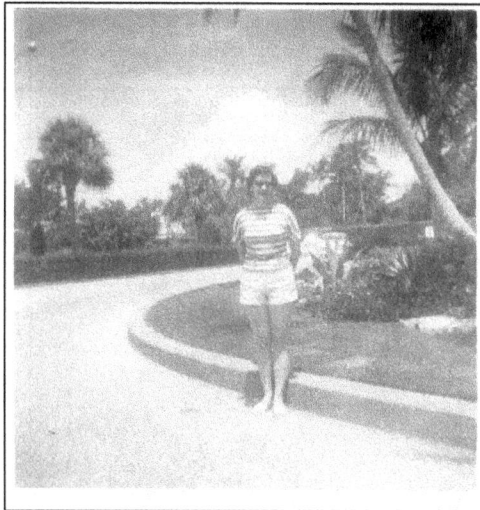

Anne Marie Gale Webb (1917-2003), Marie's 2nd daughter. She married Ocie Monroe Webb of Florida.

Grandson of Marie Gale, Dale Ernsberger (1940-2013) and wife Nancy with their two sons, Eric and Daven, about 1977.

Chris Sheffield, grandson of Marie Burrows Gale, and his bride Lisa Simon on Sept 10, 1988

Chis Sheffield's daughter, Laura with Eric Bond, on their wedding day, Dec. 5, 2015. Laura strongly favors her great grandmother, Marie B. Gale, in appearance.

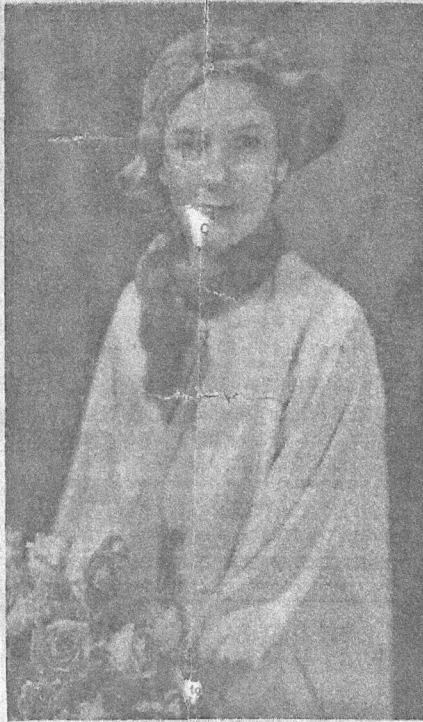

Page 24   THE NEW YORK TIMES, FRIDAY, MARCH 9, 1934.

MARION C. BLACK BECOMES A BRIDE

Member of Noted Southern Family Is Married to Regis Vaccaro in Church Here.

ESCORTED BY HER BROTHER

Donald Nash and Mrs. John Shaw Billings Attend Couple—Reception at Sherry's.

The marriage of Miss Marion Carrère Black, daughter of Mrs. Robert M. W. Black of 405 East Fifty-fourth Street and the late Rev. Dr. Black, to Regis Vaccaro, son of Mr. and Mrs. Luca Vaccaro of New Orleans, La., took place here yesterday afternoon in the chapel of St. Bartholomew's Church. The Rev. E. A. W. Hannington Wilson, rector of St. Paul's Church, Patchogue, L. I., performed the ceremony in the presence of relatives and a few close friends.

The bride was escorted by her brother, Robert K. Black of New York, who gave her in marriage. She wore an afternoon costume of blue crêpe and a hat to correspond. Her only attendant was Mrs. John Shaw Billings of New York. Donald Nash of this city was best man for Mr. Vaccaro.

A small reception at Sherry's for members of the immediate families followed the ceremony.

After a wedding trip to Nassau, Bahamas, Mr. Vaccaro and his bride will live in New Orleans, where he is associated with his father in the Standard Fruit Company and Vaccaro Brothers.

The bride is descended through her mother from the Oglethorpe family that founded the Colony of Georgia and is a descendant of General Lachlan McIntosh of Revolutionary War fame. On the paternal side she is a granddaughter of Colonel George Robison Black and a great-granddaughter of the late Edward J. Black, both of whom represented the State of Georgia in Congress. She is a great-grand-niece of the late Robert Raymond Reid, who was Governor of the Territory of Florida and who served as president of the Constitutional Convention under which Florida was admitted into the Union as a State.

MARRIED IN ST. BARTHOLOMEW'S CHAPEL. Mrs. Regis Vaccaro.

RUSSIAN GROUP HERE HOLDS BALL TONIGHT

Event at the Plaza Planned by the Georgian - Circassia Former Nobility.

THE HENRY J. PIERCES ENTERTAIN AT DINNER

Give Party in Central Park Casino—Miss Jane Erdmann Honored at Luncheon.

Aunt Ta's daughter, Marion C. Black, had a wedding announcement in the New York Times, March 9, 1934, p 24. She married Regis Vaccaro the day before. In the announcement, it stated "The bride is descended through her mother from the Oglethorpe family that founded the colony of Georgia and is a descendant of General Lachlan McIntosh of Revolutionary War fame."

Several Family Member's Obituaries

Obituaries

Gale

Mrs. Marie B. Gale, 83, of 1912 Carr St., died at her home today.

Services will be 3 p.m. Saturday at the graveside in Welaka Cemetery with Father Fred Yerkes officiating.

Mrs. Gale was the widow of William D. Gale. She had been a resident of Putnam County since 1915. Before moving to Palatka in 1935, she resided in Georgetown. She was a member of the Episcopal Church.

Survivors include two sisters, Mrs. B.H. Graham, Valona, Ga., and Mrs. Gerald Ford, Savannah, Ga.; four daughters, Mrs. G.R. Ernsberger and Miss Mary A. Gale, both of Palatka, Mrs. O.M. Webb, Florahome, and Mrs. John Sheffield, Jacksonville; five grandchildren and six great-grandchildren.

Johnson-Davis Funeral Home is in charge of arrangements.

Wright

Marie Burrows Gale's obituary ran on the day she died, July 20, 1979, in the *Palatka Daily News* and the *Florida Times Union* newspapers.

5A PALATKA DAILY NEWS •

THURSDAY, JULY 20, 2000

Clino G. Ernsberger

Clino Gale Ernsberger, 84, of Palatka, died Tuesday, July 18, 2000 at Hospice House of North Central Florida in Gainesville after a long illness.

Mrs. Ernsberger was born in Geogetown on November 15, 1915 to William Dimitry and Marie Burroughs Gale. A secretary and accountant for several corporations including: USN BUDOCKS, and General Telephone. She is a lifelong Episcopalian, former head of "Women of the Church" and Daughters of the King with her husband George Richard and sister Mary; founding members of All Saints Anglican of Palatka and Saint Michael and All Angels, Orange Park. She is the sister of Mary Gale, Anne Gale Webb, and Jean Gale Sheffield. She is the mother of two sons, Gale Richard, AE, retired design engineer NASA and Dale Dimitry, PE, CEO Engineering Associates; grandmother of five, Deborah, Margaret, Richard, Eric and Davin; great grandmother of Casey. Treasured by all who knew her.

Anglican services will be held 11:00 a.m. Friday, July 21, 2000 at Johnson-Overturf Funeral Home in Palatka with Father John Jacobs celebrant. Burial will follow in Palatka Memorial Gardens. Friends may call Friday from 10:00 to 11:00 a.m. at the Johnson-Overturf Funeral Home in Palatka.

Johnson-Overturf Funeral Home of Palatka is in charge of the arrangements.

Jean Gale Sheffield, 81, of Jacksonville, FL, passed from this life on September 13, 2008. Born November 19, 1926 to William Dimitry Gale and **Marie Burrows Gale** in Georgetown, FL, Jean was a beloved daughter, sister, wife, mother, and grandmother and will be dearly missed. Jean graduated from Putnam County High School with honors in 1945. Jean attended Tulane University in New Orleans and then later enrolled at the University of Florida where she majored in Spanish and French. She had the honor of attending UF during its first year as a coeducational university. It was during this time at school that she met John Mason Sheffield on a blind date. They wed on June 9, 1949 and were married for 58 years until John's passing in April of this year. Jean loved to travel with her family, especially to the mountains and the beach. She was also an avid reader - her favorites were mysteries and historical fiction. She also loved to write letters to her family and friends, and she sent cards for every possible occasion. The youngest of four sisters, Jean was a very devoted daughter and sister. Though her mother and sisters did not live nearby, she traveled back home for many family occasions and to care for her mother when she was ill. She was an outstanding mother, devoting her life to her daughter and two sons from childhood through adulthood. When grandchildren came along, she embraced them with love, always making them welcome and keeping their favorite treats on hand. Jean was a gentle soul with a soft, tender spirit and she will forever be in our hearts. Jean was preceded in death by her parents, her sisters, Mary Gale, Clino Ernsberger, and Anne Webb, and her husband, John. Survivors include her daughter Patricia Shuman (Mitchel), sons Lanse and Chris (Lisa), grandchildren Jennifer, Beth, Justin, Laura, and Josh, and numerous nieces and nephews The family will receive friends Wednesday, September 17, 2008 from 12:00 noon. until 2:00 p.m. at Hardage-Giddens Town and Country Chapel. Funeral Services will follow at 11:00 a.m. in the funeral home chapel. Interment will be in Riverside Memorial Park. Arrangements by Hardage-Giddens Town and Country Funeral Home, 7242 Normandy Blvd., Jacksonville, FL 32205.

Published in the Florida Times-Union from Sept. 16 to Sept.17, 2008

IZ FAGES   JJ Cents

Lewis Graham dies at young age of 97 years

Valona's Postmistress was nation's oldest

Full of life all of her 97 years, Mrs. Lewis Burrows Graham, long-time postmistress of the Valona Post Office, died Oct. 15 at Southeast Georgia Regional Medical Center in Brunswick, after being hospitalized for two weeks with a brain aneurysm.

Graveside funeral services were held Oct. 17 at Atwood Family Cemetery in Valona, with the Rev. J. Edward Harris officiating.

A native of McIntosh County, Mrs. Graham had served as the Valona postmistress for more than 20 years.

She was the first woman teller at the Citizens and Southern Bank in Savannah and she was secretary at Darien High School for many years. She had taught school at Jones, prior to working at the C & S Bank.

She attended the University of Georgia and was a member of the St. Andrew's Episcopal Church in Darien.

Surviving are two daughters, Ann G. Everett of South Daytona Beach, Fla., and Christine Lane of Darien; a son, Ben Graham of Valona; two sisters, Virginia Redding of Valona and Sybil Baker of Sea Island; six grandchildren and several nieces and nephews.

Active pallbearers were Dr. Clifford Watson, Lawrence Jacobs, Charles Phillips, Paul Johnson, Donald Forsyth, Hunter Forsyth, John A. Ream and Lynn Townsend.

Honorary pallbearers were Judge Stephen L. Boyles, Dr. James Snow, Dr. Edwin Blackburn, Bruce Ream,

Lewis Graham

Hank Ream, Reggie Sawyer, Sr., Paul Strickland, and Wesley Townsend, Sr.

Those wishing may make memorial contributions to Sanctuary on the Sapelo, Rt. 3 Box 3261, Townsend, Ga. 31331 or the American Cancer Society.

Edo Miller and Sons Funeral Home was in charge of arrangements.

From The Darien News, October 1995

Sybil W. Baker

Sybil Watson Baker, 90, of Sea Island died Tuesday, June 22, 2010, at the Brunswick hospital of Southeast Georgia Health System.

A graveside service will be held at 11 a.m. Friday, June 24, 2010, at Atwood Cemetery in Valona with the Rev. Ted Clarkson officiating.

Born March 1, 1920, in Valona to the late Thomas Perry Watson and the late Meta Atwood Watson, Mrs. Baker was a lifelong resident of McIntosh and Glynn counties.

She was a member of St. Andrews Episcopal Church in Darien and Christ Church on St. Simons Island. Mrs. Baker was a graduate of Darien High School and attended business school in Savannah.

While Mrs. Baker was a lover of the McIntosh marshes and the North Carolina mountains, nothing was more important to her than her family and friends. She was a constant source of love and encouragement.

Her love of life and the joys life provided her has served as an inspiration to all who knew her.

In addition to her parents, Mrs. Baker was preceded in death by husbands Henry Putnam Ream and Albert Brewer Baker; two grandsons, Robert Ream and Henry Putnam Ream III; two brothers, Hugh Atwood Burrows and Hunter Atwood Watson; and six sisters, Marie Gale, Lewis Graham, Claire Ford, Rita Brooks, Virginia Redding and Perry Saunders.

Survivors include her children, Hank Ream Jr. and wife Elizabeth of St. Simons Island; Priscilla Ream Parker and husband Jimmy of St. Simons Island; Johnny Ream of Sea Island, Bruce Ream and wife Patricia of Ponte Vedra Beach, Fla., Albert B. Baker III of Corpus Christi, Texas, and Steve Baker and Ronnie Taylor, both of Reno, Nev.; grandchildren, William Ream, Jennifer Ream, Sybil Kuchar and husband Matt; Drew Parker and wife Annie, Tony Ream, Putnam Ream, Claire Ream, MacIntosh Ream, Richard Ream, John Ream and wife Jenny; great-grandchildren, Cameron Kuchar, Carson Kuchar, James Parker, Lillie Ream, and Caroline Ream; and beloved family from Valona and McIntosh County. Additionally the family would like to thank Mrs. Baker's faithful caregivers, Jewel Pierce, Faye Groover, Blondell Taylor and Ann Rhodes.

In lieu of flowers, the family requests memorial contributions be made to St. Andrews Episcopal Church or Hospice of The Golden Isles.

Arrangements are entrusted to Edo Miller and Sons Funeral Home in Brunswick, GA. www.edomilerandsons.com.

Family-placed obituary
The Brunswick News June 24, 2010

4A The Brunswick News /

Monday, September 17, 2012

Carolyn H. Gorby

Carolyn Helen Watson Gorby, 65, of Darien passed away Saturday at home surrounded by her family and caretakers.

A memorial service will be held at 11 a.m. Sept. 22 at Atwood Cemetery in Valona with the Rev. Ted Clarkson officiating. A reception will follow at the family home in Valona.

She is survived by her sons, Jason Hunter Gorby of Atlanta and Brian Michael Gorby of San Francisco, Calif; three sisters, Catherine (Paul) Glenn, Virginia Baisden and Margaret (Craig) Toussaint; and a brother, Cliff (Sonja Rasmussen) Watson of Atlanta.

Carolyn is predeceased by her father, Hunter Atwood Watson, and her mother, Vivian Watson O'Kelley.

She worked as a school guidance counselor in Atlanta before returning to McIntosh County 10 years ago. She was an avid quilter, a member of McIntosh Art Association and Dorcas.

Carolyn enjoyed bright splashes of color, flower gardens, birds and tennis.

In lieu of flowers, please send donations to Hospice of Golden Isles, 1692 Glynco Parkway, Brunswick, Ga 31525.

Please sign the online registry at www.demfuneralhome.com.

David E. Miles Funeral Home of Baxley is in charge of the arrangements.

Family placed obituary
The Brunswick News September 17, 2012

111

Obituaries, Local & World

Christie Lane

Christie Lane, 60, of Townsend, Ga., entered into rest on Tuesday, Feb. 21, 2017, at Hospice of the Golden Isles in Brunswick, Ga.

Christie was born July 29, 1956, in Brunswick, Ga., the daughter of the late Wayne Pack and the late Ann Graham Everett, and lovingly raised by her grandparents, Ben H. and Lewis Burrows Graham. She was the loving wife to Gerald "Jerry" Lane. She has resided in McIntosh County for many years. Christie was a member of St. Andrews Episcopal Church in Darien, Ga.

Christie was preceded in death by her parents, Ann Everett and Wayne Pack; her grandparents, Lewis and Ben Graham; and a brother, Ben Graham.

She is survived by her husband, Gerald "Jerry" Lane of Townsend, Ga.; one son, David Lane of Darien, Ga.; a daughter, Beth Walters Parker (Ryan) of Darien, Ga.; three granddaughters, Shelby Gale, Leilani Lane and Madeline Parker; one grandson, Graham Walters; six sisters, Anita Consolatore of Ormond Beach, Fla., Melody Ross (Gordon) of Mabscott, W.Va., Ginger Liford (Keith) of Orlando, Fla., Amy Murphy (Mike) of Port Orange, Fla., Nancy Palmer (Jeff) of Coral Springs, Fla., and Susan Herhold (Shannon) of Maumee, Ohio; one brother, George Everett of Ormond Beach, Fla. Several nieces and nephews also survive.

Christie loved spending time with her family, friends and pets. She loved her grandchildren and cherished their time spent together. She also enjoyed cooking, collecting antiques and family gatherings. Christie loved to travel, spending time camping and boating. She will be missed by all who knew and loved her. Her family will have many fond memories to cherish for years to come.

The family will receive friends between the hours of 6-8 p.m. Friday, March 3, 2017, at Edo Miller and Sons Funeral Home.

A memorial service to honor her life will be held at 11 a.m. Saturday, March 4, 2017, at St. Andrews Episcopal Church in Darien, Ga. Father Ted Clarkson will officiate the service.

Memorial contributions can be made in Christie's memory to the Saint Andrew's Episcopal Church Parish House Fund or Hospice of the Golden Isles.

Arrangements are entrusted into the care of Edo Miller and Sons Funeral Home, www.edomillerandsons.com.

Family-placed obituary
The News, March 1, 2017

112

Benjamin Wayne Graham

Darien, Georgia native Benjamin Wayne (Ben) Graham drifted to his final rest on Thursday, January 26, at the age of 61.

Born on April 1, 1955 to Wayne Pack and Ann Douglas Graham, he was lovingly raised by his grandparents, Ben and Lewis Graham.

It may be that Ben learned his approach to life from the water. He grew up next to it, earned his living on it; it framed his days. Its ebb and flow was reflected in him. Ben could be quiet, and drift along like the river on a quiet day. Or he could be passionate and fierce, like a sudden storm over the Atlantic. His slow drawl, his radiant smile, and his easy laugh will be greatly missed by many friends and companions.

Ben is survived by his sisters, Christie (Jerry) Lane, Anita Consolatore, Melody (Gordon) Ross, Jr., Ginger (Keith) Liford, Amy (Mike) Murphy, Nancy (Jeff) Palmer, and Susan (Shannon) Herhold; a brother, George Everett; nieces, Beth Walters-Parker, Rachel and Christina Ross, Valorie and Amy Consolatore, and Paige Ellis; nephews, David Lane, Gordon Ross, III, Lee Consolatore, Michael Murphy, Atticus Palmer and Saxon Litz; great-nieces Shelby Gale and Leilani Lane; and great-nephew Graham Walters.

A memorial service is planned for Tuesday, Feb. 7 at 11 a.m. at St. Andrew's Episcopal Church in Darien, Georgia. All friends are welcome to attend.

In lieu of flowers, the family is asking that contributions in Ben's name be made to the St. Andrew's Episcopal Church Parish House Building Fund. From *The Darien News*, Feb. 2, 2017

7 CORRESPONDENCE AND DOCUMENTS

Included in this section:

John M Atwood's 1931 statement re his Atlanta property

My dear Mete letter from Maud, with family history

My dear little Clara letter, Civil War era letter of a soldier to his wife, presumably Clara LaRoche

Two letters to Hunter A. Watson from his paternal aunt, Ruth Watson, regarding Watson family history

Manchester deed, McIntosh County, GA, 1875

Warranty deed, Hudson Tract, 1905

Ann M Atwood Will, 1873

Ann M Atwood Estate Inventory, 1925

Ann M "Meta" Watson Will, 1957

Wedding license, 1908, TP Watson and Ann M "Meta" Burrows

John M. "Gran" Atwood's statement of what happened to his Atlanta Real Estate, page 1 of 4.

"The following is a true statement dictated by my father, John M. Atwood.

Dec. 20 1931 - West End property was apportioned to my sister Matilda Hopkins and myself 1/2 to each. I gave my nephew, Geo K. Camp, power of atty. to sell <u>one</u> <u>lot</u> in West End, Atlanta, and he sold <u>my</u> <u>entire</u> <u>interest</u> to_all that property 25/48 skipped out west. Rather than prosecute my nephew, his father Geo. Camp Sr. begged me to accept five hundred dollars and drop the suit - this was only a fractional part of what the property was worth.

In the division of my Mothers Estate, I was awarded "Hudson Tract"; containing about 900 acres with 200 or 300 acres marsh; 3 Hammocks; and Patterson Island with several hundred acres of marsh lands - Also other wild land." *(continued on next page)*

John M. "Gran" Atwood's statement of what happened to his Atlanta Real Estate, page 2 of 4.

"I also had an interest in some farm land in Greene and Putnam counties. Also in Sumpter Co. some city lots, and farm lands in latter. Brother Alf, (J.A. Atwood,) was supposed to own ½ Int. in Sumpter Co. lands. The other ½ interest was supposed to be <u>mine</u>, but I got nothing out of it."

"My Mother gave me this land also McIntosh Co. land, a <u>life interest</u> <u>in it.</u> Also same <u>life</u> <u>interest</u> in other property, but Executor's sold it, without consulting me, and I got <u>nothing</u> out of it! They said they needed the money and, had the power, (as Executors) to sell any land they wanted to." *(continued on next page)*

John M. "Gran" Atwood's statement of what happened to his Atlanta Real Estate, page 3 of 4.

"Division of my Mothers Estate was made after I became of age, during her lifetime or most of it was apportioned off then. When I failed in Mercantile business at Crescent, it became necessary to sell some land to raise money for my creditors. The Hudson Tract was sold at public outcry auction before doors of Court House bought in with my children's Mothers money (for them) by A.H. Brown, and deeded to them, Geo. E. Atwood appointed guardian."

"It was at this time to protect my heirs (children's) rights to the tract of land known as "Manchester", or Clark's tract, that I agreed to deed my ½ interest in same, to my brother George, temporarily, he assuring me he would make deed back to me soon as safe,- but he died suddenly without doing this." *(continued on the next page)*

John M. "Gran" Atwood's statement of what happened to his Atlanta Real Estate, page 4 of 4.

"To show that he recognized (sic) my interest in this land, I deeded several lots to Julie & Janie in Valona - had he considered I had no interest in this land, he would have deeded it to them, himself, disregarding me. George's heirs only made a deed to 35 acres, after his death, to me, tho I was entitled to ½ of Clark Tract or "Manchester" and marshes; my children are entilled [sic] to ½ Interest in this Tract after my death". I don't care to have any unpleasantness about this during my lifetime.

Signed John M. Atwood

(In the) Presence of Meta A. Watson (and) Clara Black - May 10, 1928"

My Dear Mete letter

The original letter follows. This undated handwritten letter was found in the papers of Virginia Redding by her daughter-in-law, Suzanne Durant Forsyth. It provides the family lineage from Donald McKenzie through his daughter Anna McKenzie, Anna McCullough, and Ann Margaret Mable McIntosh. Since it is addressed to "Mete" and is talking about Ann and Henry Atwood as "Our Grandparents," I assume this letter was sent to my grandmother, Ann Margaret "Meta" Atwood Burrows Watson, possibly in the 1940s or 1950s.

Sky(?) Valley Camp(?)
June 12th
My dear Mete - I have been trying to go through all these papers & Maurie's Aunties & little Sibyls until my head is fussled.- I hope what I have found will help you a little in the family records area way, but I do not think they will help to join the Col. Dames, as Donald McK_ was not granted enough land and his date was not old enough, They have changed it all since Cousin Hattie(?) and Sally West (got) in. Miss Maude Heyward(?) in Savh., genealogist for Colonial Dames, wrote me quite a few letters some time ago, & she advised me to join in Conn. & be transferred or through Mamie's ancestors but I gave up. It was so much (work?). & after cousin Hattie(?) said they had lost their papers by fire - I would not bother, but now I am sorry I did not go on farther in it for this sake, but I do not think she cares- Ward(?) would have been pleased for me to be a Dame. Hope you are O.K. I hear is awfully hot down in Charleston. It is usually so up here & it is a beautiful spot.

I never could get Jaime(?) Heyes(?) wife to even ans. my letters, of course she should not have that old Grant or other valuables of ours, but she will not answer any letters. I can not see why she would want these things. I seem to remember Maurie & me copying more than this record, especially about the McKenzies

I will try & write down what I have for you. Lovingly Maud

[Editor's note: this is the page following the handwritten letter]
In 1765 Donald McKenzie was granted by King Geo III, 200 acres of land in Ga. province, Cedar Point and so on- He married Mary Merriman and their only daughter Anne married John McIntosh, their son John L. McI_ married Margaret McCullough, she died soon, leaving an infant, Anne   Margaret, who her grandmother McI_ raised. - Mrs. McI_ lived to be 109 years old at

Cedar Point where she died. Anne Margaret married Henry Skilton Atwood who came from Conn originally. They were married in Darien Wed. eve-Dec. 7th 1824- They were our Grandparents- She had 9 children it says.

The Atwoods came to Conn. from England If I can look up anything more I will be glad to try. I suppose you know as much as I do about the Conn. Atwoods. I would like to know more about the McKenzies- too bad we did not look into all this years ago, before Papa died & Mamie could have helped us more- young people do not seem to care about these things until it is too late –

(Editor's note: Anna McKenzie lived to be 100 years old; also some family records say Donald McKenzie, while others say Daniel McKenzie)

"My dear Mete" actual handwritten letter, page 1 of 4

in. Miss Maud Howard
Genealogist for Col. Davis, in Sark.
wrote me quite a few
letters some time ago &
she advised me to Davis
in Conn. & be thankful
of through Mamie's ancestry
but I gave up it was
so much [illegible] &
the Cousin Hatts said
they had lost their papers
by fire - I would not
bother, but now I am
sorry I did not go on
further in it for his
sake, but I do not
think she cares - had
would have been pleased
for me to be a Davis,
Hope you are O.K.
I know it is awfully

"My dear Mete" letter, page 2 of 4

"My dear Mete" letter, page 3 of 4.

In 1765 Donald McKenzie was granted by King Geo. III, 200 acres of land in Ga. Province. Cedar Point and so on — He married Mary Merriman and their only Daughter Annie married John McIntosh, their son John L. McI married Margaret McCullough she died soon, leaving an infant, Anne Margaret, who her grand mother. McI raised — Mrs. McI lived to be 109 years old at Cedar Point where she died — Anne Margaret married Henry Skilton Atwood who came from Conn originally. They were married in Glorious Wash. eve — Dec. 7th 1824 — They were our Grand parents — She had 9 children it says.
The Atwoods came to Conn. from England & I can look up any thing more I will be glad to try. I suppose you know as much as I do about the Conn. Atwoods. I would like to know more about the McKenzies — Too bad we did not look into all this years ago, before Papa died & Mamie could have helped us more — Young people do not seem to care about these things until it is too late —

"My dear Mete" letter, page 4 of 4.

Corinth Miss
May 17th, 1862

My dear little Clara

Your box arrived yesterday — a very delightful present it proves. The cake, one of them, was cut and eaten in a trice. It was long since some of the feeders had indulged in such luxuries.

The mosquito box is just the thing. The mosquitos are not so thick yet but flies are very troublesome and I revel under almost the only box in Corinth — Thanks to my dear little wife-

No battle yet and no change except that all officers are forbidden correspondence on army movements —

The enemy have not yet taken Vicksburg — the people having nobly determined to be shelled before submitting —

Well, I wish the war was over — I am heartily tired of this life.

~*~

Family letter from the Civil War, as seen in the Darien High School yearbook of 1963 or 1964. The original letter has since been misplaced. Actual image of letter in yearbook follows. Presumably this letter was written to Clara LaRoche as she is the only Clara in the family that would've been a young wife during the Civil War.

William McIntosh

James Spalding

Two letters to Hunter Watson from Thomas Perry "TP" Watson's Sister-in-law Ruth. TP was the father to Ann Margaret "Meta" Atwood's last five children, including Hunter. Postmark of 6 Aug 1974 for the first letter.

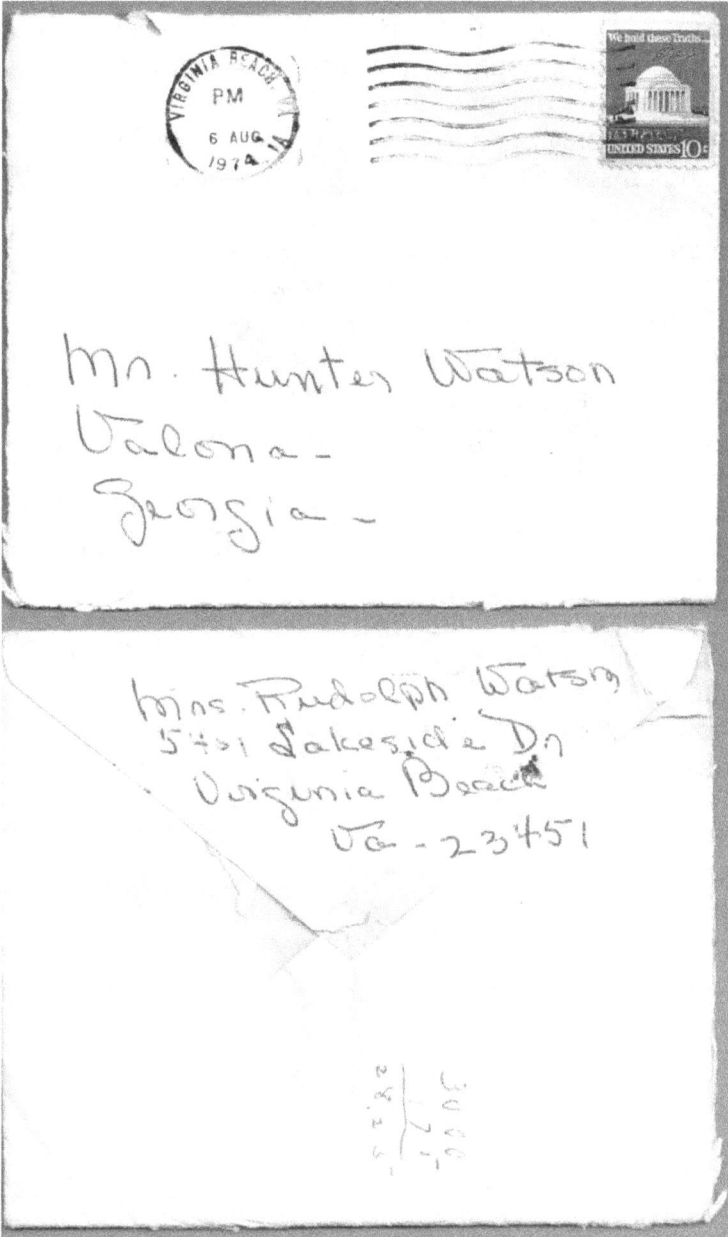

Dear Hunter,

I must write you the sad news of Rudy's death on June 30th. He had been ill for a long time and had been in the hospital and convalescent home since February. Rudy was eighty-eight years of age and lived a healthy and happy life. This does not make parting easy but it is some comfort. I am grateful for our own son Roddy and his two children. You know you are the oldest of this generation and Roddy is the youngest, the only ones to carry on the name of Watson. Roddy has a son, Stockton Tyler Watson. Wish you could know each other.

You may not know that Charlotte Watson of Colonial Beach [Virginia] died. She is the one who was the historian in the family. I'm afraid we have missed our chance of getting some family facts. Her sister Louise still lives at the Beach, so perhaps she has some of Charlotte's papers. I hope you will be coming this way some time as you did some years ago. I would love to see you all.

I am trying to forget these weeks of Rudy's illness (he did not suffer) and to remember all the beautiful times we had. I am living in the same house, and, of course, it is very lonely. Roddy is about five minutes away which helps.

Your family must be grown up by now. I would love to have some news of you all.

I hope you will get this. I am only guessing at your address.

My love to all of you.
Affectionately,
Aunt Ruth
8th August

~*~

[Second letter from Ruth to Hunter Watson, which follows]

Dear Hunter,

I am enclosing a copy of "Watson History" which Berkeley Moore has gathered. I thought you and your family would be interested. There may be some names which could be clarified, but I think it is fairly accurate.

While I have not been too well recently, I am better now. This is a difficult adjustment and I have a real understanding of those who have gone through this.

Do hope you and yours are well. I loved your letter and your children sound interesting.

Roddy is, of course, my main help in making a new way of life and he is a real joy to me.

For the time being, I shall stay in our home. My brother who lives in California [California, Maryland] will be spending more and more time with me, I hope.

Dearest love to you all,
Aunt Ruth
Dated 18 November.

~*~

The handwritten letters follow, along with the typed Watson family history.

Dear Hunter,

I must write you the sad news of Rudy's death on June 30th. He had been ill for a long time and had been in the hospital and convalescent home since February. Rudy was eighty-eight years of age and lived a healthy and happy life. This does not make the parting easy but it is some comfort. I am grateful for our son Roddy and his two children. You know you are the oldest of this generation and Roddy is the youngest, the only ones carrying on the name of Watson. Roddy has a son, Stockton Tyler Watson. Wish you all knew each other.

You may not know that Charlotte Watson of Kelmia Brown died. She is the one who was the historian in the family. I'm afraid we have missed our chance of getting some family facts. Her sister, ~~Charlotte~~ Louise still lives at the Bonds, so perhaps she has some of Charlotte's papers.

August 1974 letter from Ruth Watson to her nephew Hunter Watson, page 1 of 2

130

I hope you will be
coming this way some
time as you did some
years ago - I would
love to see you all.
I am trying to
forget all those weeks
of Rudy's illness (he
did not suffer) and

to remember all the
beautiful times we had.
I am living in the same
house and of course,
it is very lonely. Reddy
is about five minutes away
which helps.
Your family must
be grown up by now.
I would love to have
some news of you all.
I hope you will
get this - I am only
guessing at your address.
My love to all of
you.
Affectionately
Aunt Ruth
8th August.

August 1974 letter from Ruth Watson to her nephew Hunter Watson, page 1 of 2

Dear Hunter,

I am enclosing a copy of "Watson History" which Berkeley more than gathered. I thought you and your family would be interested. There may be some names that could be clarified but overall it is fairly accurate.

While I have not been too well recently, I am better now. This is a very difficult adjustment and I now have a real understanding of those who have gone thru this.

Do hope you and yours are well. Steele

Your letter and your children
sound most interesting —

Roddy is, of course, my
main help in making a
new way of life. and is
a real joy to me

For the time being I shall
stay on in our home — My
brother who lives in California
will be spending more and
more time with me, I hope —

Dearest love to you
all —

Devotedly
Aunt Ruth —

15th November —

WATSON HISTORY

1. James Watson m. Mary Greene of the family of General Nathanael Greene of Revolutionary War fame. General Greene retired in Georgia and after his death Eli Whitney, inventor of the cotton gin, lived on the plantation and tutored the children.

2. Joseph Watson settled in southern Maryland, probably in southern Charles or St. Mary's County. He was of Scotch descent and took an active part in the early religious and political life of the county in which he lived. He had three wives - Dent (issue below), Cooke, and McPherson.

3. Roderick Greene Watson of "Clifton", Charles County, Maryland. Married Ann Perry, daughter of Thomas Perry of Charles County, county surveyor and member of state legislature, lived at "Blossom Point". There were fifteen children, six of whom died in infancy. Surviving were:

   1. Roderick Dhu m. Zorah Posey and their issue are the Leonardtown, Maryland, Watsons.

   2. Sarah Elizabeth (Sally).

   3. Mary Augusta (Molly) m. Dr. Carvell, no issue.

   4. Sterling d. when a young man.

   5. Samuel Dent m. Mary Ashton and had three daughters. Charlotte, Louise and Virginia. Louise is the only surviving one, now living at Colonial Beach, Virginia.

   6. Susan Frances (Floddie).

   7. Charles Gales - unmarried.

   8. Rudolph b. 1852, m. Sarah Northen of "Riverview", King George County, Virginia (see issue below).

   9. William Dent - unmarried.

   The children of Rudolph and Sarah Watson are as follows:

      1. Thomas Perry m. Meta Atwood
      2. Taliaferro Hunter m. Jean Sturdevant
      3. Margaret m. Lee Hiatt
      4. Carolyn Belle m. Alexander Moore
      5. Rudolph m. Ruth Wingate

Sept. 1974

Watson history provided to Hunter Watson by his Aunt Ruth (Mrs. Rudolph Watson of Virginia Beach, 1974.

Copy of Deed. Pg 1. (Copied from "Book" G."
Pg." 373'- McIntosh Court House.

This indenture, made this August, 1896, between Rut A. Dunwoody of Bibb County, Ga., Geo. H, and Jane M. Camp, of Coop County, Ga.; Wm Henry, James Alfred, + John M. Atwood, of McIntosh County, Ga., parties of the first part, + Geo. E. Atwood, of McIntosh County, Ga., party of the second part: Witnesseth, That in or about the year 1875– an agreement was made and entered into, between all the parties above mentioned, whereby the tract of land in McIntosh County, Ga. known as "Manchester," hereinafter and more fully described, was valued at Two Thousand Dollars ($2,000.00) and it was determined that the said George E. Atwood and John M. Atwood, or either of them, should have the privilege of buying the same at said price of $2000.00 and that titles should be made to them, upon payment to the other parties, above named, of their pro-rata, of said sum of $2000.00 and whereas the said Geo. E. Atwood in the year of 1882 made same payment, on account, and has since then fully satisfied(?) the said parties of the first part, but no titles have ever

Handwritten copy of Manchester deed from McIntosh County Courthouse, Book G, page 373, of agreement made in 1875, from Virginia Redding collection

135

Second page of hand-copied deed, related to the Manchester Tract, from Virginia Redding collection

Page 1 of 3 of Warranty deed for 500 acres from part of the Hudson tract, 1905, from the Virginia Redding collection

To Have and to Hold the said *bargained Land*
with all and singular the rights, members and appurtenances thereunto appertaining, to the only proper use, benefit and behoof of *G. E. Atwood in trust for Mary L. & Ann Margaret Atwood* the said *G. E. Atwood in trust for Mary L. and Ann Margaret Atwood their* heirs, executors, administrators and assigns, in FEE SIMPLE : and the said *A. H. Brown*

the said bargained *Land has*

unto the said *G. E. Atwood in trust for Mary L. and Ann Margaret Atwood their* heirs, executors, administrators and assigns, against the said *A. H. Brown his* heirs, executors and administrators, and against all and every other person or persons, shall and will warrant and forever defend by virtue of these presents.

In Witness Whereof, The said *A. H. Brown*
ha *s* hereunto set *his* hand, affixed *his* seal, and delivered these presents, the day and year first above written.

Signed, Sealed and Delivered in presence of us :

C. C. Dean
R. W. Brewster
Notary Public for
McIntosh Co.

A. H. Brown (Seal)

Page 2 of 3 Warranty Deed for 500 acres from part of the Hudson tract, dated 1905, from the Virginia Redding collection

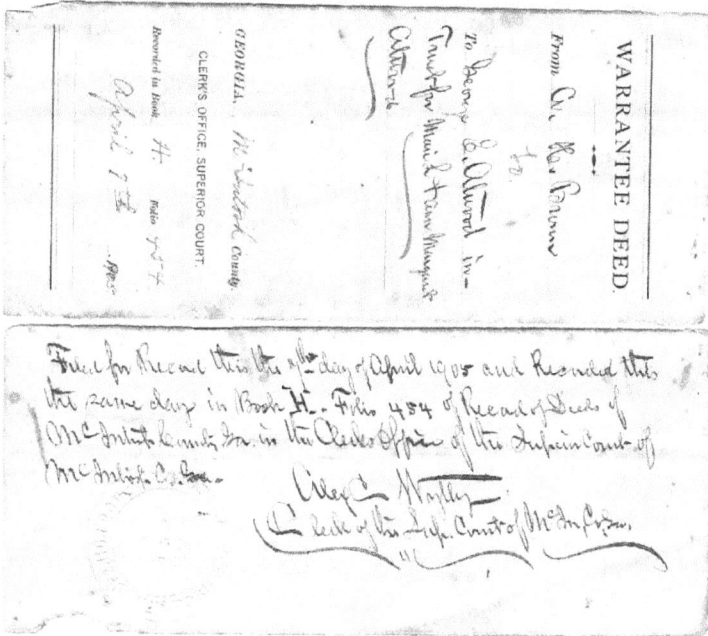

Page 3 of 3, Warranty deed for 500 acres from part of the Hudson tract, dated 1905, from the Virginia Redding collection

GRANTORS:		KIND OF INSTRUMENT:
		Last Will and Testament and Codicil
Ann M. Atwood, Testatrix		WHERE EXECUTED: Georgia, Putnam County.
		DATE: Will....... July 2nd, 1867. Codicil.....March 27th, 1873.
GRANTEES:		CONSIDERATION: . . . .
		DATE OF RECORD: Not given
		PLACE OF RECORD: Ordinary's Office Putnam County, Ga. Will BOOK C PAGE 164,165,166 163
WHEN ACKNOWLEDGED OR PROBATED: May 5th, 1873. ACKNOWLEDGED OR PROBATED BEFORE: D. H. Reid, Ordinary in Common Form.		WITNESSES: [CODICIL] [WILL] C. P. Shepard, E. S. Williams H. P. Nichols, S. I. Owens, A. N. Simpson. A. P. Brady."

DESCRIPTION OF PROPERTY:

"Item 1st. I appoint my sons, William Henry and James A. Atwood, Executors of this my last Will and Testament.

Item 2nd. With the exceptions, qualifications and conditions hereinafter stated, I give, devise and bequeath all of my property, both real and personal to be equally divided between my sons and daughters who may be living at the division of the same, and to them only, not intending hereby that there shall be any representative of a son or daughter who may be deceased at the time of said division by any child or children, the offspring of said son or daughter deceased.

Item 3rd. I wish my property to be divided when my youngest child shall come of age. In the meantime I direct that my Executors shall hold the same for the support and maintenance and education of my youngest children and also for the support and maintenance of my daughters, Matilda A. Atwood, so long as she remains unmarried, unless she should defer marriage until after the period hereinbefore fixed fro the distributing of my estate.

Item 4th. Being joint owner with my son, James A. Atwood of certain real estate in Sumter County in said State, upon which there is a Mill and as my son, James A., may have a choice and preference in the matter of the son who is to take my interest in said property under this Will, it is proper, I think that he should have the privilege of designating which one of his brothers shall take my place as joint owner with him. I therefore will that said interest shall be set-off in said division to whichever of my sons my son, James A. shall choose to be associated with him and if the value of the property so set-off shall exceed a distributive share of my estate then I direct that the son so taking said property shall pay the excess to the other distributees.

PAGE

WEAVER & CRAVEN
ATTORNEYS AT LAW
GEORGIA CASUALTY BLDG.
MACON, GA.

Last Will and Testament of Ann M. Atwood, dated July 2, 1867 and revisited with a codicil in March 27, 1873, page 1 of 2, from the Virginia Redding collection

Item 5th. Certain silverware distributed share and share alike.

[CODICIL]

The Testarix recites the foregoing Will and her intention to change it in the following particulars:

" In the first place my daughter Matilda A. Atwood, who afterward married Charles Hopkins, Jr., having departed this life, leaving no child or children of her body, I hereby bequeath all the of the property mentioned in my will and testament as bequeathed to my said daughter Matilda A. Atwood, to be divided share and share alike , among the surviving beneficiaries of my said last Will and Testament.

Secondly. I hereby alter and change all those items, sections and parts of my said last will and testament whereby property therein mentioned is be-queathed to my sons William H. Atwood, James A. Atwood, and George E. Atwood, and to my daughters, Ruth A. Dunwoody and Jane M. Camp and to my grand-daughter, Ann Margaret Geiger so that my said sons William H. Atwood, James A, Atwood, John M. Atwood and George E. Atwood and my said daughters Ruth A. Dunwoody and Jane M. Camp and my said grand-daughter Ann Margaret Geiger, shall each have and enjoy only a life interest in the property mentioned in my said Last Will and Testament as bequeathed to each of them, with remainder over after the death of each one of them to the children of their bodies in fee simple, but should any one or more than one of my said legatees die, leaving no child living child, then remainder over in after the death of such a one or more than one without issue in fee simple to the surviving beneficiaries of my said last Will and Testament to be divided share and share alike among them"

Last Will and Testament of Ann M. Atwood, dated July 2, 1867 and revisited with a codicil in March 27, 1873, page 2 of 2, from the Virginia Redding Collection

No.1.   Inventory and Appraisement of Property
of the Estate of Mrs Anne M. Atwood.
(deceased)

One mule "Kit" value . . . . $ 50.00
  "   "   George   " 80.00
Half interest in two mules 70.00
One mare 25.00
  "   2 horse wagon 50.00
  "   old Carriage 25.00
Half interest in phaeton 75.00
15 7/8 shares Roseville Factory stock
    (In Cobb Co.) . . . . $ 4700.00
Prefered stock Roseville Mfg Co.
  $ 97.00 per share . . . . $ 5-69.87
28 Shares Cap'tl. stock Central R.R.
    and Brokerage Co. . . . . $ 2240.00
32 Shares Cap'tl Stock Ga. R.R.
    & Brokerage Co. . . . . $ 2870. 00
                                            2870. 00
Lot of Seed Cotton 50.00
One old Carriage body 5. 00
                                       $ 10009.00

**Estate Inventory of the late Ann Margaret Atwood,
1925, page 1 of 5, from the
Virginia Redding Collection**

Pg. no. 2.

Georgia, Putnam Co. } We do certify that as far as was produced to us the foregoing contains a just and true appraisement of Mrs Anne M. Atwood; late of said County, deceased, to the best of our skill & judgment, this August 20th 1873. signed;

"J. O. Rosser" }
"2 S. Owen" }
"K. D. Little" }

Georgia, Putnam Co. }

I do certify that 2. S. Owen, K. D. Little & Jno. O. Rosser, appraisers of the Estate of Mrs Anne M. Atwood, late deceased, were sworn by me to perform as appraisers according to Law. --
This Aug 20. 1873.
Wm D. Little J. P.

Estate Inventory of the late Ann Margaret Atwood,1925, page 2 of 5, from the Virginia Redding Collection.

Greene County, Georgia.

Georgia.
Putnam Co } Greene County:

A just and true Appraisement of all the Goods and Chattels, of Mrs Anne M. Atwood, deceased, late of Putnam Co., Ga.

as produced to us, by W.H. and J.A. Atwood, Executors, of the Estate of the said Mrs Anne M. Atwood, deceased..

99/800 of Oconee Mills, which embraces the Factory; Store house; Operative Houses, and all other buildings, and 500 acres of land,— more or less,—total amt. appraised by us, at $ 30.000.00 — 99/800 is $ 3 712.50

I hereby certify above appraisers } Jno. D. Copland.
have taken the oath required } Jno. Curtright.
by law, on this Aug 26th 1873. } Reuben A. Cridille.
Reuben A. Cridille, N.P.,
Greene Co., Ga.

Estate Inventory of the late Ann Margaret Atwood, 1925, page 3 of 5, from the Virginia Redding Collection.

Estate of Mrs Anne M. Atwood.
McIntosh County, Georgia.
Sept. 9th, 1873.

Appraisement of the property of Mrs
Anne M. Atwood, late of Putnam Co. Ga.
We do hereby certify that having
been duly appointed appraisers, of certain property, consisting of Wild Land
in McIntosh Co.—

One half-interest in three (3) City
Lots, in Darien, Ga., and one half
interest in one mule, the following
is true value of said property, to
the best of our judgment, all being
the property of Mrs Anne M. Atwood,
late of Putnam Co, deceased.

500 acres Wild Land, more or less $ 100.00
½ Interest in three City Lots 75.00
½ " " One mule 50.00
$ 225.00

Sworn to and subscribed before me,
this 9th day of September, 1873.
Alec Wylly, N.P.
& Ex. off. J.P.

J. A. La Roche,
R. McDonald.
W. F. Gibson
appraisers

**Estate Inventory of the late Ann Margaret Atwood,
1925, page 4 of 5, from the
Virginia Redding Collection**

Estate Inventory of the late Ann Margaret Atwood, 1925, page 5 of 5, from the Virginia Redding Collection

My last will and Testament,
May 9 – 1957

Description of property

Item 1st. I appoint my son's Hunter A. Watson; Hugh A. Burrous and Henry P Ream, Executors of this my last Will and Testament.

I give devise and bequeath all my property realy personal to be devided between my following childrens children, (or my grand-children.)

I direct that my Executors shall hold the same until my grandchildren shall come of age unless they get married. but my grand daughter Sybel Watson Saunders can not sell the home place—I now live on—but can live on it herself, but it is not to be conveyed to anyone else nor sold, ever! Should she marry a man that my sons esteem a good match, and able to support her well She can come into possission on her

Ann Margaret "Meta" Watson's will, 1957, p 1 of 3,
Virginia Redding Collection

(2)

25" birthday - title to be made to her for her life time, and then go to children of her body - should she die without leaving an heir (her own son or daughter), title will revert to my grand-daughter's, Virginia and Margaret Watson; share & share alike;

I bequeath to Gay Saunders Jacobs, one half acre, in the field, back of my home (a little to the south of my home) -

I bequeath to my grand son, Donald M. Forsythe - at my death (or before it) 1/2 of enclosure he fenced in, bounded N, by road; East, by road; South by field;

West by road; At Hugh Burrow's death the 1/2 of Doris field goes back to Don. M. Forsyth, (in other words, Hugh a Burrow has only a life interest, in the part he has (a vegetable garden in - at present.)

**Ann Margaret "Meta" Watson's will, 1957, p 2 of 3,
Virginia Redding Collection**

(3)

Claire B. Ford, my daughter, is to have
a small lot in field, west side acre,
also Lewis B. Graham to have a small
lot, fronting on West road about ½ acre
near Claire's lot & south of Don M. Forsyth's
lot, but bounded on North by Don's property.

All these little land lots are not
to be sold to any one, but kept
for their child or children at their
death, if sale has to be made the
surviving brothers of Don M. Forsyth
or his uncles, aunts or cousins, have preference or his mother, Virginia W Forsyth,
this is in case any of the grantees
die without children of their bodies.

**Ann Margaret "Meta" Watson's will, 1957, p 1 of 3,
Virginia Redding Collection**

Thomas Perry Watson's marriage license to Meta Burrows on March 6, 1908. Accessed online through Ancestry.com, Georgia Marriage Records from Select Counties, 1828-1978

8 SOURCES

Ancestry.com, Church of the Latter Day Saints, DAR Records, FindAGrave.con, Genealogy.com, Rootsweb — various official documents of births, deaths, and marriages.

Cemeteries of McIntosh County, Georgia, Lower Altamaha Historical Society, 2000, edited by Mattie R. Gladstone

L'Engle, Gertrude N., A Collection of Letters, Information and Data on Our Family, 1949, Vol. II.

Personal papers from the estate of the late Virginia Redding of McIntosh County, GA, provided by her daughter-in-law Suzanne Forsyth, Valona, GA

Reports of Cases Determined in the District Courts of Appeal in Georgia, Vol 14, from Decatur Term (1853) to Columbus Term (1854) inclusive, Thomas R. R. Cobb reporter, digitized book, originally published by Reynolds and Brother, Athens, GA, 1854, pp 404-438.

Scots of McIntosh, Lower Altamaha Historical Society, undated, edited by Lillian B. Schaitberger, 15 pages, printed by *The Darien News*.

Sullivan, Buddy, *Early Days on the Georgia Tidewater*, 1990, published by the McIntosh County Board of Commissioners

The Atwood Family and Allied Families, 28-page booklet, author unknown, publication date unknown

ABOUT THE AUTHOR

Margaret Watson Toussaint writes nonfiction under her name. She published *Remembering*, a memoir about family times in Valona during the summer of Hurricane Dora, and a prior limited edition version of this Family History. She also wrote feature articles for *The Darien News* in Darien, GA, for about ten years. Prior to her writing career, she was a contract scientist for the U.S. Army at Fort Detrick, Frederick, MD. She writes fiction under the pen name of Maggie Toussaint.

Southern author Maggie Toussaint writes mystery, suspense, and dystopian fiction. Her work won the Silver Falchion Award for best mystery, the Readers' Choice Award, and the EPIC Award. She's published seventeen novels as well as several short stories and novellas. Maggie serves on the national board for Mystery Writers of America, is currently President of Southeast Mystery Writers of America, and is Co-VP of LowCountry Sisters In Crime. Visit her at www.maggietoussaint.com

www.ingramcontent.com/pod-product-compliance
Lightning Source LLC
Chambersburg PA
CBHW051426090426
42737CB00014B/2854